Studies in Honor of

Albert Morey Sturtevant

GREENWOOD PRESS, PUBLISHERS
WESTPORT, CONNECTICUT

Copyright 1952 by the University of Kansas Press

Reprinted by permission of
the University of Kansas Press

First Greenwood Reprinting 1970

Library of Congress Catalogue Card Number 76-100163

SBN 8371-3967-8

Printed in the United States of America

Contents

	Page
INTRODUCTION L. R. Lind	3
THE PHONEMES OF MODERN ICELANDIC Kemp Malone	5
THE SYNONYMS FOR "SEA" IN *BEOWULF* Caroline Brady	22
COMPOUNDS OF THE *MANN-SKRATTI* TYPE Stefán Einarsson	47
THE RUNES OF KENSINGTON Erik Wahlgren	57
TWO UNRECOGNIZED CELTIC NAMES Lee M. Hollander	71
THE IMPACT OF ENGLISH ON AMERICAN-NORWEGIAN LETTER WRITING Einar Haugen	76
ON THE ORIGINAL OF THE CODEX REGIUS OF THE ELDER EDDA Didrik Arup Seip	103
MELKÓLFS SAGA OK SALOMONS KONUNGS Jess H. Jackson	107
WILHELM GRIMM'S LETTERS TO PETER ERASMUS MÜLLER P. M. Mitchell	119
THE PROBLEM OF CATHOLIC SYMPATHIES IN SWEDISH ROMANTICISM Adolph B. Benson	138
ALBERT MOREY STURTEVANT: BIBLIOGRAPHY OF PUBLICATIONS L. R. Lind	162

Studies in Honor of
Albert Morey Sturtevant

Introduction

μικρὸν ἀντίδωρον ἀντὶ τῆς μεγαλοψυχίας δίδομεν

For more than forty years the name of Albert Morey Sturtevant has appeared in the front rank of American scholarship. During this period he has steadily and patiently produced an imposing series of important studies in the wide field of Scandinavian and Germanic philology and literature. His special interests have lain in the region of Norwegian, Swedish, Gothic, and Old Icelandic phonology, etymology, morphology, syntax, and literature. In his philological work he has emphasized the articulation between dialects and the interrelations of the Germanic and classical languages, as in his researches on the language of the Gothic Bible; in literature, he has been attracted to the religious and aesthetic elements particularly in the writings of Ibsen and Tegnér. He has sought to leave nothing in isolation but has studied his materials with a vision of their importance as parts of a whole; in all his investigations, whether of syntax or semantics, he has kept the spirit as well as the letter before him, the perfect, shining whole which must rise from the scattered fragments.

His rigorous standards of scholarship, his genial spirit, and his uncompromising honesty have won him deserved recognition at home and abroad. Since 1920 he has ably edited a first-class journal, *Scandinavian Studies,* the official publication of the Society for the Advancement of Scandinavian Study in the United States, and has made it a leading avenue of publication for the best scholarship in its field. His name is well known to scholars abroad; it is mentioned more frequently than that of any other American in such standard works as Andreas Heusler, *Altisländisches Elementarbuch,* and Sigmund Feist, *Vergleich-*

INTRODUCTION

endes Wörterbuch der Gotischen Sprache (third edition, 1939). In the latter Professor Sturtevant's name appears only in the sections which indicate by eight-point type the fact that the etymologies listed in them are the most accurate available. In the *Svensk Litteraturhistoria* of Schück and Warburg he is praised highly for his numerous essays on Esaias Tegnér, the Swedish poet.

It is, therefore, to a distinguished scholar that the present volume of papers composed in his honor is offered. The papers are not limited strictly to the areas of his own competence but range widely over Scandinavian civilization in its literary and philological aspects. The University of Kansas Press and the Committee for the Humanistic Series (C. K. Hyder, Chairman; L. R. Lind; James Seaver; and W. H. Shoemaker; the Committee has been greatly assisted by J. A. Burzle, Chairman of the Department of German, and by J. N. Carman, former Chairman of the Committee) are proud to bring forth such a tribute to one of the University's most important teachers, now in well-earned retirement but as productive as ever. For as a teacher, Professor Sturtevant has always exemplified, with all of Tegnér's *"kraft och klarhet,"* those qualities of spirit which, as he himself says of Tegnér in "An American Appreciation of Esaias Tegnér," drew him irresistibly to the Swedish poet: "his refinement: refinement of soul, of intellect, and of literary feeling; his humanitarian ideals; and his modesty."

The writer of this introduction now adds his heartfelt wishes to those of his colleagues that a friend and scholar so gifted and fortunate may live long and publish many more contributions to the understanding of Scandinavian culture.

L. R. LIND

The Phonemes of Modern Icelandic

KEMP MALONE

Johns Hopkins University

SINCE THE PUBLICATION, in 1923, of my monograph *The Phonology of Modern Icelandic*,[1] a new linguistic discipline, that of phonemics, has won general recognition; or perhaps it would be better to say that the study of sound-systems is now sharply differentiated from ordinary phonetics. In my book of 1923 it was my concern to isolate, describe, and exemplify the sounds used in modern Icelandic speech, but in so doing my approach was phonetic rather than phonemic. In the present paper I take account of work done since 1923, of course; in particular, I have profited by study of Professor Stefán Einarsson's volume *Icelandic*.[2] But I have been chiefly concerned to present the Icelandic sound-system in strictly phonemic terms. In other words, I have tried first of all to classify each isolable speech-sound as an allophone of some phoneme. In the process I have had to deal with not a few problems which the phonetician need not consider. I can only hope that my treatment of these problems will prove convincing to my fellow-workers in the field, or will stimulate them to find better solutions.

I begin with the stops. The Icelandic system of stops consists of twelve surds (i.e., voiceless phonemes); no vibrants (i.e., voiced phonemes) occur. The system of stops takes shape as follows:

STOPS	velar	palatal	dental	labial
aspirated	k	k̑	t	p
short unaspirated	g	g̑	d	b
long unaspirated	g:	g̑:	d:	b:

The aspirated stops are always short. In the speech of southern and western Iceland, including Reykjavík, oppositions such as the following establish the system of stops given above:

kappi hero and *kjappi* he-goat [kah:bɪ, ǩah:bɪ]
gá look and *gjá* chasm [gau:, ǵau:]
Sigga proper name and *siggja* (gen. pl.) callus [sɪg:a, sɪǵ:a]
káfa fumble and *gáfa* gift [kau:va, gau:va]
kista chest and *gista* spend the night [kɪs:da, ǵɪs:da]
vaka wake and *vagga* cradle [va:ga, vag:a]
skekja shake and *skeggja* (gen. pl.) beard [sǵe:ga, sǵeǵ:a]
tala speech and *dala* dent [ta:la, da:la]
gata street and *gadda* spike [ga:da, gad:a]
peð pawn and *beð* bed [pe:þ, be:þ]
slapa hang loose and *slabba* lounge [sla:ba, slab:a]

Note however that the short-long oppositions involve two factors: the length of the stop and that of the preceding sonant, a short stop regularly going with a long sonant and a long stop with a short sonant.

In the northern and eastern speech area the system of stops consists of eight phonemes only, as the factor of length is allophonic rather than phonemic, the short and long unaspirated stops being in complementary distribution. Thus, the word-pair *vaka-vagga*, which appears as [va:ga, vag:a] in south and west, takes the form [va:ka, vag:a] in north and east, where the short member of the short-long opposition is an aspirated stop. So far as the factor of length is concerned, the two speech areas agree perfectly here, but they differ in that the opposition [va:ka, vag:a] is qualitative as well as quantitative, whereas the corresponding [va:ga, vag:a] of south and west is quantitative only.

The stops show the following pattern of distribution. The aspirated stops occur in all dialects in initial position. Examples: *kalla* call, *kvöld* evening, *ker* tub, *trega* mourn, *par* pair, *planta* plant, *prestur* priest. In the speech of north and east they also occur after a long vibrant. Examples: *aka* [a:ka] ride in a vehicle, *fálki* [faul:kɪ] falcon, *at* [a:t] fight, *samt* [sam:t] yet, *api* [a:pɪ] ape. The short unaspirated stops occur initially, after initial [s], and after a long consonant. Examples: *brenna* burn, *skeið* [sģei:þ] spoon, *mynda* [mɪn:da] shape, *ást* [aus:d] love, *helga* [hel:ga] hallow. Examples peculiar to southern and western speech: *fálki* [fau̯l:ģɪ] falcon, *samt* [sam:d] yet; in north and east the corresponding words have long vibrants followed by aspirated stops (see above). The short unaspirated stops also occur after a long sonant in southern and western speech. Examples: *aka* [a:ga] ride in a vehicle, *at* [a:d] fight, *api* [a:bɪ] ape. The long unaspirated stops occur only after a short sonant; in consequence, they do not occur initially but they do occur medially and finally. Examples: *höggva* hew, *beinn* [beid:ṇ] straight, *bolli* [bod:lɪ] cup, *afl* [ab:l̩] strength, *dögg* dew. In compounds, and in foreign words pronounced as if they were compounds, the rules for initial position apply to each element. Examples: *handklæði* [-klai:þɪ] towel, *apótek* [-te:g] pharmacy.

The Icelandic system of nasals takes shape as follows:

Nasals	tectal	dental	labial
surds	ŋˢ:*	ṇ	m̥:
short vibrants		n	m
long vibrants	ŋ:	n:	m:

A tectal, be it understood, is a phoneme made against the tectum or roof of the mouth. Icelandic has both velar and palatal nasals, but they are not separate phonemes, as are the corresponding stops, but mere allophones of the tectal nasals. Both the tectals are always long and the long mark set after them is therefore not strictly needed, but it serves to give the oppositions below a more balanced look and to remind the reader of the factor of length which makes part of these phonemes. The dental surd may be

---

* Typographical difficulties make it needful to represent surd n in this way; the superscript ˢ means "surd."

[7]

either long or short, but here we have to do with allophones, in complementary distribution, not with separate phonemes. The long allophone is so marked in the oppositions given below. The labial surd is always long, so far as I can find, except in the colloquial *lasm,* short for *lagsmaður* chum; in my system of nasals I have ignored this isolated case. The labial surd and the corresponding short vibrant are in complementary distribution, but the two differ so greatly in phonetic quality (and quantity) that one is hardly justified in making them mere allophones of a single phoneme. Phonemicists who do not agree with me on this point will of course change accordingly the system of nasals outlined above.

In the speech of southern and western Iceland such oppositions as the following bear out the system of nasals just given:

lengt (pp.) lengthened and *lengd* length [leiŋ˳:d, leiŋ:d]
hnegg neighing and *negg* heart [n̥eg:, neg:]
grant exactly and *grand* harm [gran̥:d, gran:d]
men necklace and *menn* men [me:n̥, men:]
eymt (pp.) galled and *eymd* misery [eim̥:d, eim:d]
ama vex and *amma* grandmother [a:ma, am:a]
megnt (neut.) strong and *meint* hurt [meiŋ˳:d, mein̥:d]
langs (gen.) long and *láns* (gen.) loan [lauŋ̊:s, laun̥:s]
gegnt (pp.) obeyed and *geymt* (pp.) kept [ǵeiŋ˳:d, ǵeim̥:d]
gangs (gen.) gait and *ǵams* (gen.) glutton [gauŋ̊:s, gaum̥:s]
kennt (pp.) taught and *kembt* (pp.) combed [ḱen̥:d, ḱem̥:d]
lön hayrick and *löm* hinge [lö:n̥, lö:m̥]
kenndi (pret.) taught and *kembdi* (pret.) combed [ḱen:dɪ, ḱem:dɪ]

In the speech of northern and eastern Iceland the long surds characteristic of the south and west do not occur, the long vibrants being used instead. In this dialect, then, there are only six nasal phonemes. The oppositions given above hold for north and east, however, as may be seen in the following:

lengt (pp.) lengthened and *lengd* length [leiŋ:t, leiŋ:d]
grant exactly and *grand* harm [gran:t, gran:d]
eymt (pp.) galled and *eymd* misery [eim:t, eim:d]

[8]

Here the phonemes in opposition are not surd and vibrant nasals but aspirated and unaspirated stops. In other cases the glottal articulation of the nasals plays no part in the opposition, whatever the dialect. Examples for north and east:

megnt (neut.) strong and *meint* hurt [meiŋ:t, mein:t]
gegnt (pp.) obeyed and *geymt* (pp.) kept [ǵeiŋ:t, ǵeim:t]
kennt (pp.) taught and *kembt* (pp.) combed [ḱen:t, ḱem:t]

These word-pairs show both vibrant nasals and aspirated final stops, as against the surd nasals and unaspirated stops of south and west, but the oppositions depend on another factor, the place of articulation, in all dialects.

Before certain phonemes a nasal may have a loose oral articulation, a greater or less degree of opening instead of the stoppage found elsewhere. Examples:

tungl [tuŋ:l] moon
aðeins [a:þeins] only
vingsa [viŋ:sa] waft
einhver [eiŋ:xøɹ] someone
langt [lauŋ:t, lauŋˢ:d] long

But these nasal spirants, if one may so call them, are not separate phonemes but mere allophones of the ordinary nasals, those made with oral stoppage. A dental stop has no such loosening effect on a preceding homorganic nasal. Before a pause a short vibrant nasal commonly loses its vibrancy in the course of its articulation; it begins as a vibrant but becomes a surd before the articulation is over; a phoneme so made I call a spent vibrant. Examples: *kom* came, *hún* she. The variation between full and spent vibrancy is allophonic, not phonemic, and therefore needs no further attention here.

The nasals show the following distribution. The tectals do not occur in initial or final position, but the vibrant may occur in sandhi if the next word begins with a tectal. Example: *Jón*

Grímsson. In such cases, however, the vibrant is hardly a member of the tectal phoneme but serves as an allophone of [n]. Within a word the vibrant may occur before a short unaspirated tectal stop. Examples:

ganga [gauŋ:ga] go
gengi [ɟeiŋ:ɟɪ] good luck

In the speech of northern and eastern Iceland, it may occur likewise before an aspirated tectal stop. Examples:

banka [bauŋ:ka] knock
banki [bauŋ:kɪ] bank

In the speech of south and west these words have the surd tectal nasal followed by an unaspirated stop. The tectals may likewise occur before certain dentals. Examples:

unglings [uŋ:liŋs] of youth
ungt [uŋˢ:d, uŋ:t] young
þyngd [þiŋ:d] weight

The short dental surd occurs initially and finally but not medially: its long allophone occurs only in medial position. Examples: *hneppa* [neh:ba] button, *vatn* [vah:dn̩] water; *beint* [bein̩:d] straight. As we have seen, the long surd is peculiar to the speech of south and west; it occurs before a short unaspirated stop. In composition or sandhi the final surd keeps its surdness if the next word or word-element begins with a surd. Example: *jafnfætis* [jab:n̩fai:dɪs] on all fours (with).

The short dental vibrant occurs initially, medially, and finally. Examples: *nef* nose, *búnaður* farming, *hefna* avenge, *sýn* sight. In medial position it occurs between sonants and after a consonant but not before a consonant, except as the first member of the sequences [nsg, nsd]. Examples: *danska* Danish, *enskt* [ensd] English (neut.). The long dental vibrant does not occur initially but it occurs medially and finally. Examples: *Anna* Ann,

THE PHONEMES OF MODERN ICELANDIC

hand [han:d] hand, *hann* [han:] he, him. In medial position it occurs between sonants and before but not after a consonant. Apart from the word *lasm* mentioned above, the labial surd nasal occurs neither initially nor finally; it occurs medially before a short unaspirated stop in the speech of south and west. Examples: *lampi* lam̥:bɪ] lamp, *rúmt* [rum̥:d] roomy (neut.). The short vibrant occurs initially, medially, and finally. Examples: *mál* speech, *saman* together, *pálmi* palm, *tóm* vacuum. In medial position it occurs between sonants and after a consonant, but not before a consonant except as the first member of the sequences [msg, msd]. Examples: *heimska* folly, *blómstur* bloom. The long labial vibrant occurs medially and finally. Examples: *remma* bitterness, *lamb* [lam:b] lamb, *skömm* [sgöm:] short (fem.). In medial position it occurs between sonants and before but not after a consonant.

The Icelandic system of liquids is as follows:

Liquids	trill	side
surds	ɹ̥	l̥
short vibrants	r	l
long vibrants	r:	l:

The surds may be either short or long but this difference is allophonic rather than phonemic. The following oppositions bring out the system of liquids given above:

hreykja lift and *reykja* smoke [r̥ei:ga, rei:ga]
orka strength and *orga* howl [or̥:ga, or:ga]
vera be and *verra* (neut.) worse [ve:ra, ver:a]
hlaða barn and *laða* attract [l̥a:þa, la:þa]
milti milt and *mildi* mildness [mɪl̥:dɪ, mɪl:dɪ]
kali ill will and *Kalli* Charlie [ka:lɪ, kal:ɪ]
böl misfortune and *böll* (pl.) dance [bö:l, böl:]

The liquids are all dentals. In words like *ljós* bright and *rjett* rightly there is more or less palatalization, but the variation is allophonic, not phonemic. The various phonemes have the fol-

[11]

lowing distribution. The short allophone of the surd trill occurs initially, as in *hrafn* raven, and finally under weak stress, as in *kaldur* cold (masc.). It does not occur medially except as the first member of the sequences [r̥sg, r̥sģ, r̥sd]. Examples: *bernska* [ber̥sga] childhood, *ferskja* [fer̥sģa] peach, *fyrst* [fir̥sd] first. The long allophone occurs medially before [s], as in *vers* verse, and before a short unaspirated stop, as in *korkur* cork, *partur* part, and *harpa* harp.

The short vibrant trill occurs initially, medially, and finally. Examples: *reka* drive, *klifra* climb, *svara* answer (verb), and *svar* answer (noun). It may also be heard medially in words like *barn* [bardn̥] child and *varla* [vardla] hardly, though more commonly it is lost in this position. Finally before a pause it is a spent rather than a full vibrant. The long vibrant does not occur initially or finally. It occurs medially between sonants, as in *herra* gentleman, before a short unaspirated stop, as in *margur* many, and before a vibrant consonant, as in *garður* garden.

The short allophone of the surd lateral phoneme occurs initially, as in *hló* laughed, and finally after long stop or [s], as in *fjall* [fjad:l̥] mountain, *gafl* [gab:l̥] gable, *tagl* [tag:l̥] horse tail, *hvísl* [xis:l̥] whisper. The long allophone occurs medially before a short unaspirated stop. Examples: *túlka* [tul̥:ga] interpret, *malt* [mal̥:d] malt, *skálpur* [sgaul̥:bø̥r] sheath. Note that the opposition *milti-mildi* given in the table of oppositions above holds for all dialects.

The short lateral vibrant occurs in initial, medial, and final position; when final its vibrancy is spent rather than full before a pause. Examples: *leka* leak, *boli* bull, *illa* [id:la] badly, *kringla* [kriŋ:la] circle, *fölsk* (fem.) false, *helzt* [helsd] preferably, *hel* hell. The long vibrant occurs medially and finally, as in *milla* ornamental loop, *milljón* million, *ball* dance. It occurs chiefly before a consonant, as in *pylsa* sausage, *síld* herring, *silfur* silver. In northern and eastern speech it occurs also in words like *túlka* interpret and *skálpur* sheath, where the south and west have the surd lateral.

The fricatives of Icelandic, classified by place of articulation, fall into velars, palatals, gingivals, dentals, and labials. The distinction between surd and vibrant is phonemic for palatals and labials; that between short and long, for the gingivals. The Icelandic system of fricatives therefore takes shape as follows:

Fricatives	surd	vibrant	short	long	undifferentiated
velar					x
palatal	ç	j			
gingival			s	s:	
dental					þ
labial	f	v			

Oppositions such as the following establish this system of fricatives:

hjá by, with and *fá* get [çau:, fau:]
hjól wheel and *jól* Yule [çou:l, jou:l]
hjer here and *hver* hot spring [çe:r, xe:r]
hjalli ledge and *salli* dust [çad:lı, sad:lı]
hjú servant and *þú* thou [çu:, þu:]
fax mane and *vax* wax [fax:s, vax:s]
furt churl (acc.) and *jurt* herb [før:d, jør:d]
feta step and *seta* seat [fe:da, se:da]
hosa hose and *hossa* toss [ho:sa, hos:a]
hvar where and *þar* there [xa:r, þa:r]
hvetja whet and *setja* set [xe:dja, se:dja]
kaffi coffee and *kassi* box [kaf:ı, kas:ı]

The velar fricative occurs in initial, medial, and final position. The initial allophone, *hv* in conventional orthography, is a short surd, usually but not necessarily pronounced with lip-rounding. Many Icelanders substitute [kv] for it, a pronunciation which gives rise to a number of homophones, as *hver* hot spring and *kver* pamphlet. The medial allophones are written variously in conventional spelling: in most cases with *g*, but in words

[13]

THE PHONEMES OF MODERN ICELANDIC

like *lax* [lax:s] salmon the phoneme is combined with [s], the sequence [x:s] being represented by a single symbol; before *t* and *s* the phoneme may be written *k̬*. A medial allophone may be short or long, surd or vibrant. The short surd occurs before [s] plus stop, as in *vöxtur* [vöxsdǫr̥] growth; also before [l̥d], as in *siglt* [sɪxl̥d] sailed (pp.). The long surd occurs before a surd consonant, as in *flygsa* [flɪx:sa] rag, *slíkt* [slix:d] such. The short vibrant occurs between sonants, as in *saga* [sa:xa] history, and before [ld], as in *sigldi* [sɪxldɪ] sailed (pret.) The long vibrant occurs, or may occur, before a vibrant consonant, as in *daglega* [dax:le:xa] daily, *sagði* [sax:þɪ] said (pret.), *fagra* [fax:ra] fair (acc.), but before most such consonants it occurs in composition only. The final allophone of [x] is regularly a short spent vibrant, as in *lög* [lö:x] law.

The palatal surd fricative is always short and occurs in initial position only; see the examples in the table of oppositions above. The corresponding vibrant is likewise always short; it occurs initially and medially but not finally. In conventional orthography it is usually represented by *j* but not infrequently by *g*. Examples:

jú yes
bjartur bright
bljúgur bashful
brjef letter
djarfur bold
drjúpa drip
fjall mountain
fljóta float
frjáls free
gljá glitter
grjón grits
hljóð sound
hnjé knee
hrjóta fall
hylja hide
kljúfa cleave

krjúpa kneel
kveðja greeting
ljett lightly
lygi [li:jɪ] lie
mjólk milk
njóta use
pjátur pewter
prjóna knit
rjúfa break
rýja fleece
sjálfur self
skrjáfa rustle
slepja slime
sljettur flat
smjör butter
smyrja smear

snjallur eloquent
spjót spear
stjórn government
strjúka stroke
stynja sigh
syfja get sleepy
tjald tent
trje tree
týgi [ti:jɪ] gear
vjel machine
þjóð nation
þrjóta fail
ægja [ai:ja] frighten
ægilega [ai:jɪle:xa] awfully

Though I class [j] with the fricatives, it is markedly open in its oral articulation and little friction is heard; it might well be called a semivowel instead. Note that the letter *j* is used as a spelling device to mark *k* or *g* as representing a palatal stop. Examples: *kjósa* [ḱou:sa] choose, *gjald* [ǵal:d] payment, *rekja* [re:ḱa, re:ǵa] unwind, *rekkja* [reh:ǵa] bed. In such cases, of course, *j* does not represent a separate phoneme. Similarly with the spelling *hj* for [ç], as in *hjarta* [çar̥:da] heart.

Both the short and the long gingival fricatives are always surd. The short occurs in initial, medial, and final positions. Examples: *segl* sail, *gjósa* gush, *lás* lock. Initially it may also occur before a consonant, as in *sjón* sight, *skák* chess, *slengja* fling, *smiður* smith, *snara* snare, *spá* prediction, *stafa* spell, *svartur* black; before two consonants, as in *skrá* list, *sljór* stupid, *smjúga* creep, *snjór* snow, *spje* mockery, *spretta* spring, *stjarna* star, *strá* straw; and before three consonants, as in *skrjóður* worthless old book, *strjáll* scattered. Medially it may occur not only between sonants but also at the head of a consonant group, as in *eystra* [eisdra] in the east; between consonants, as in *fylgsni* [fɪlsnɪ] hiding-place; and after a consonant, as in *dansa* [dan:sa] dance. Finally, it may occur after a consonant as in *sax* [sax:s] knife, as well as after a sonant (see above).

The long gingival fricative occurs only in medial and final position. Medially it occurs between sonants, as in *byssa* [bɪs:a] gun, and before a consonant, as in *kasta* [kas:da] cast, *rusl* [røs:l̥] rubbish, *lasna* [las:na] decay. Finally it occurs only after a sonant, as in *fúss* discontent. Note the opposition *grís* [gri:s] pig, *gríss* [gris:] pig's.

The dental fricative may be either surd or vibrant, but this variation is not phonemic. The initial allophone, written þ in conventional orthography, is regularly a short surd. Examples: *þjófur* thief, *þungur* heavy, *þvinga* compel. In a few words like *það* that, the allophone becomes vibrant under weak stress. The short medial allophone is a vibrant; it occurs between sonants, as in *meðan* [me:þan] while, and after a consonant, as in *sagði* [sag:þɪ] said (pret.). There are two long medial allophones: a vibrant, which occurs before a consonant, as in *heiðni* [heiþ:nɪ] heathen times; and a surd, which may (but need not) occur before *ḳ*, as in *maðkur* [maþ:gø̞r̥] maggot. The final allophone is a short spent vibrant. It occurs after a sonant, as in *leið* [lei:þ] way, and after a consonant as in *sigð* [sɪx:þ] scythe. In conventional orthography *ð* is the symbol for the medial and final allophones, but phonemic transcription requires but one symbol for all allophones.

The labial surd fricative may be short or long. The initial allophone is short. Examples: *faðir* father, *fjöður* feather, *flagg* flag, *fljót* river, *fregn* news, *frjáls* free. The short medial allophone occurs before [s] plus stop and before [l̥d], as in *egypskur* [e:ɡɪfsgø̞r̥] Egyptian, *efstur* [efsdø̞r̥] topmost, *eflt* [efl̥d] furthered (pp.); in *tromfa* [trom:fa] trump (verb) it occurs after a consonant. The long allophone occurs between sonants (in words of foreign origin) and before a surd consonant. Examples: *skúffa* [sguf:a] drawer, *slifsi* [slɪf:sɪ] necktie, *loft* [lof:d] air, *rífka* [rif:ga] enlarge, *dýpstur* [dif:sdø̞r̥] deepest. In *offra* [of:ra] offer it occurs before a vibrant consonant. In final position the phoneme may be either long or short; it is short in *tromf* [trom:f] trump (noun), long in *eff* [ef:] letter name.

The corresponding vibrant phoneme may be short or long. The initial allophone is always short, as in *vaða* wade, *vje* temple. A short medial allophone occurs between sonants, before [ld], after a liquid, and after short or long [g]. Examples: *gefa* [ǵe:va] give, *efldi* [evldɪ] furthered (pret.), *álfur* [aul:vø̞r̥] elf, *gervi* [ǵer:vɪ] guise, *sökkva* [söh:gva] sink, *söngvari* [söyŋ:gvarɪ] singer, *Tryggvi* [trɪg:vɪ] proper name. A long medial allophone

THE PHONEMES OF MODERN ICELANDIC

occurs before a vibrant consonant or [g]. Examples: *kefja* [kʼɛv:-ja] dip, *vafði* [vav:þɪ] wrapped (pret.) *sífra* [siv:ra] grumble, *lífga* [liv:ga] revive. The final allophone is a short spent vibrant, as in *ef* [e:v] if, *þörf* [þör:v] need, *gólf* [goul:v] floor.

One might well include the aspirate [h] among the fricatives, but I have chosen to treat it separately. In Icelandic it occurs in two positions: immediately before and immediately after the sonant of its syllable. In the first of these positions it is always short; in the second, always long. The long allophone is further restricted in position: it occurs only between a short sonant and a short unaspirated stop. Oppositions such as the following establish the short allophone:

hey hay and *grey* hound [hei:, grei:]
hundur hound and *sundur* asunder [høn:døʀ, søn:døʀ]
hæja relieve and *bægja* hinder [hai:ja, bai:ja]

Similarly for the long allophone:

skatt (acc.) tax and *skaft* shaft [sgah:d, sgaf:d]
kapp zeal and *karp* carping [kah:b, kaʀ:b]
bakki bank and *barki* windpipe [bah:ɡɪ, baʀɡɪ]
átt direction and *ást* love [auh:d, aus:d]
hattur hat and *haltur* lame [hah:døʀ, hal̪:døʀ]
satt (neut.) satisfied and *sagt* (pp.) said [sah:d, sax:d]
nótt night and *nógt* (neut.) enough [nouh:d, noux:d]

Both allophones are surds. In the conventional spellings *hj*, *hl*, *hn*, *hr* the *h* does not represent a separate phoneme; the digraphs represent the surds [ç, l̥, n̥, r̥] respectively. For *hv* see above, under "fricatives."

So far, we have dealt only with the consonants of Icelandic. The sonants fall into two groups: vowels and glides. The vowel system of Icelandic takes shape as follows:

Short	back	mean	front	Long	back	mean	front
close	u		i	close	u:		i:
open	o	ø	ɪ	open	o:	ø:	ɪ:
low	a	ö	e	low	a:	ö:	e:

[17]

Short-long oppositions such as the following establish the system given above:

fúss displeasure and *fús* ready [fus:, fu:s]
íss (gen.) ice and *ís* (nom.) ice [is:, i:s]
bolla bun and *bola* (acc.) bull [bol:a, bo:la]
munnur mouth and *munur* difference [mön:ör̥, mö:nör̥]
hinn (masc.) the and *hin* (fem.) the [hɪn:, hɪ:n]
banna forbid and *bana* (acc.) slayer [ban:a, ba:na]
rögg energy and *rök* (pl.) reason [rög:, rö:g]
spenna clasp and *spena* (acc.) nipple [sben:a, sbe:na]

Note that the oppositions involve consonants as well as sonants, a short sonant going with a long consonant and vice versa.

I add a few short-short oppositions for the record:

súld damp weather and *síld* herring [sul:d, sil:d]
forða save, *furða* wonder, *firða* (gen.pl.) distance
stakkur stack, *stökkur* brittle, *stekkur* fold
fúss discontent, *foss* waterfall, *fass* (gen.) gait
und wound and *önd* duck [ön:d, ön:d]
filla (acc. pl.) elephant, *filla* halibut skin, *fella* fell

Likewise a few long-long oppositions:

bútur stub and *bítur* fox [bu:ðör̥, bi:ðör̥]
holur hollow, *hulur* (pl.) veil, *hylur* pool
var aware, *vör* lip, *ver* case
lúða halibut, *loða* cling, *laða* attract
stuðull prop and *stöðull* milking pen
vígur skilled in arms, *vigur* spear, *vegur* way

The glides of Icelandic behave like the vowels and are best taken up in the same connection. The Icelandic system of glides is as follows:

SHORT GLIDES				LONG GLIDES			
open-close	ou		ei	open-close	ou:		ei:
low-close	au	öy	ai	low-close	au:	öy:	ai:

Short-long oppositions like those listed below bear out this systematization:

[18]

flónni (dat.) the flea and *flóni* (dat.) fool [floun:ɪ, flou:nɪ]
meiss (gen.) creel and *meis* (nom.) creel [meis:, mei:s]
hárri (dat.) high and *hári* (dat.) hair [haur:ɪ, hau:rɪ]
dauss (gen.) deuce and *daus* (nom.) deuce [döys:, döy:s]
færri fewer and *færi* (subj.) bring [fair:ɪ, fai:rɪ]

I add the following short-short oppositions:

nótt night and *neitt* anything [nouh:d, neih:d]
sangur singed, *söngur* song, *sængur* (pl.) bed [sauŋ:gør, söy-, sai-]
þótt although and *þátt* (acc.) section [þouh:d, þauh:d]
eistur (pl.) stone and *æstur* vehement [eis:døɹ, ais:døɹ]
rósta brawl and *rausta* (gen. pl.) voice [rous:da, röys:da]
feng (acc.) catch of fish and *föng* (pl.) hold [feiŋ:g, föyŋ:g]

Finally, I give a few long-long oppositions:

bón request and *bein* bone [bou:n, bei:n]
lána lend *launa*, reward, *læna* rill [lau:na, löy:na, lai:na]
mór peat and *már* gull [mou:r, mau:r]
neyða compel and *næða* blow [nei:þa, nai:þa]
róða rood and *rauða* yolk [rou:þa, röy:þa]
seiður sorcery and *sauður* sheep [sei:þøɹ, söy:þøɹ]

Phonetically speaking, this does not exhaust the list of Icelandic glides, but the glides left out are not phonemes but mere allophones of long vowels. Thus, *lygi* mendacium may be pronounced not only [lɪ:jɪ] or [li:jɪ] but also [lii:jɪ], with a glide [ɪi:] which is an allophone of [ɪ:] or [i:]. Similarly, [oi:] serves, not as a phoneme in its own right but as an allophone of [o:] in words like *bogi* [bo:jɪ, boi:jɪ]. Again, *lifa* live (verb) may be pronounced either [lɪ:va] or [lɪe:va]. In the space at my disposal I cannot undertake to set down all these allophones, or to specify the conditions under which they occur. For a good though short discussion, see S. Einarsson, *Icelandic*, pp. 4 ff.; here the material is not presented in phonemic style, but the phonemicist can determine for himself which glides (or diphthongs, as Einarsson calls them) are phonemes and which are allophones of long vowels.

Limitations of space likewise keep me from taking up in any detail the distribution of the sonantal phonemes. A few general observations will have to do. The long sonants occur in stressed syllables only. Icelandic stress may be initial, medial, or final. The first syllable of a word takes initial stress; the stress that falls on a monosyllable may also be called initial. This is the strongest stress; weak words may lose it in the sentence, with consequent shortening of the sonant. Medial stress falls on the first syllable of the second element of a composite word; a heavy suffix, too, may take medial stress. Final stress falls on the syllable before a pause; e.g., the last syllable of a sentence. Within these limits long sonants occur. They are further restricted to open syllables and to syllables that end in one short consonant.

In dividing a word or word-element into syllables, a short consonant between sonants goes with the second sonant; so also a twosome (i.e., sequence made up of two consonants) which consists of a short stop or an [s] plus [j] or [r] or [v]. Examples: *eta* eat, *etja* incite. A long consonant between sonants goes with both; that is, it ends one syllable and begins the next, the syllabic boundary dividing it into two unequal parts; I say "unequal" because the first part takes most of the length; indeed, a long consonant between sonants is better called overlong, since its first part, taken alone, is fully long. A long consonant before another consonant goes with the preceding sonant. Examples: *missa* lose, *missti* lost (pret.).

The short sonants of Icelandic occur (1) before long consonants, (2) before heavy consonant groups made up of short consonants, and (3) in unstressed syllables. Example for (1) and (3): *brennimark* brand. Here all three sonants are short: *e* and *a* because each comes before a long consonant, and *i* for want of stress. Example for (2) and (3): *efstur* topmost. Here both sonants are short: *e* because it comes before the heavy consonant sequence *fst*, and *u* for want of stress.

Each individual sonant has a variety of allophones. Thus, [e] is nasalized in *menta* educate, and is a spent vibrant in *keppa* contend. But I have already stretched my allotment of space to the utmost, and I must make an end.

REFERENCES

1. New York University, Ottendorfer Memorial Series of Germanic Monographs, No. 15.
2. Johns Hopkins Press: Baltimore, 1945; second ed., 1949.

The Synonyms for "Sea" in *Beowulf*

CAROLINE BRADY

Marion Talbot Fellow, 1952-53

THAT THE VOCABULARY of the Old English poet abounds in synonyms—for sea and sword, king and warrior, battle and hall, God and demons, as well as for any number of other concepts in the worlds of nature and of man—and that no inconsiderable number of these words and locutions, especially the nominal compounds and genitive phrases, are "figurative or partially figurative," "metaphorical," "pictorial" are beliefs so firmly established in the critical literature as scarcely to invite dispute. Yet certain questions still await answers: In what way and to what extent are the words and phrases within the several groups synonymous; that is, do the poets actually use them as synonyms, in any currently accepted sense of that term? How many of these words and locutions are demonstrably genuine metaphors, and how many perhaps metonymical or synecdochic but strictly literal in their reference in their actual contexts? Do all the poets use the same words in exactly the same meanings; or are differences discernible, historical as well as personal? that is, is it possible that not only were some poets more discriminating than others in their choice and use of diction, but also some words experienced changes in meaning, through usage or from other causes, in the course of the period during which the poets were writing? Further investigation of these and related questions will require a re-examination of a substantial part of the vocabulary of Old English poetry; but it will reveal more than we now can know not only about the power and the artistry of the individual poets, but also about the changes of meaning, nonfigurative as well as figurative, which actually took place in

THE SYNONYMS FOR "SEA" IN *Beowulf*

Old English, and possibly something of the dates when these changes took place.

The present investigation deals with a single group of words —simple and compound nouns and genitive phrases referring to the sea, its various aspects, its parts, and its characteristics—in a single poem, *Beowulf*.[1] The purpose is twofold: to determine whether or not this poet actually uses a total of forty words and phrases as synonyms, all (or nearly all) with the general meaning of "sea";[2] to discover, so far as is possible, which of these really are or contain figures of speech—in particular, metaphors—and which are literal in their application, appellatives or terms descriptive of their referents in whole or in part, relating properly to the sphere of experience to which the referent belongs. Throughout the analysis we proceed from the actual contexts, and all the contexts, in which the terms appear. The lists of isolated words and phrases occurring in glossaries and most of the special studies of this sea-vocabulary[3] serve useful purposes; but even when they are accompanied by explanations of the primary or essential meanings of the individual words and the differences between them, they do not enable us to determine with any degree of precision the meanings the *Beowulf* poet may have wished to convey, for they present the words in a vacuum, lacking definite objective reference.[4] We note the adjectives used attributively with the nouns because, remarkably few in this poem and seldom purely conventional, they for the most part serve to fit more precisely to the contexts the nouns which they restrict. Of equal importance in determining the meanings of the nouns are the verbs used with them; also sometimes of special significance are the prepositions.

References to water occur in thirty-one of the forty-four sections of the poem;[5] but not all of these are to the sea. The *wæter-egesan* of l. 1260 and its variation *cealde stréamas* in l. 1261 serve

[23]

solely to characterize Grendel's mother as a water-monster, with reference to no specific body of water. The passage describing the hilt of the ancient sword with which Béowulf killed Grendel's mother (ll. 1687-1698) contains four words used of the sea elsewhere in the poem, but here used of the Flood: *flód*; *gifen*, modified by *géotende*; and *wæter* and *wylm*, in the phrase *wæteres wylm*. The *flódes wylm* (l. 1764) of Hróðgár's lengthy moral discourse very probably, but not necessarily, refers to the sea: it is a generality, without specific reference, standing in a list with *fýres feng* and *gáres fliht*. In l. 2546 *wælm* refers, not to the ocean, but to the bubbling of a burn (*burnan wælm*), the *stréam* of l. 2545, from the dragon's barrow. The *wæter* of ll. 2722, 2791, and 2854 is literally "water," with which Wígláf bathes and seeks to revive the dying Béowulf. So also is the *wæter* of l. 93 (*swá wæter bebúgeð*) best taken as "water," even though the poet uses the same construction with *sǽ* occupying the position here held by *wæter*; for there (l. 1223) he is speaking of the sea surrounding the inhabited earth, here, in the Song of the Creation, of the waters under the heaven in the midst of which God let the dry land appear. In the accounts of the wars between the Swedes and the Geats, *sǽ* (l. 2380), *síd sǽ* (l. 2394), *wæter* with an adjective, presumably *wíd* (MS: *rid*) (l. 2473), and *hæf* (l. 2477) refer to the expanse of water between the two peoples—that is, Lake Väner (and Vätter?), not the sea. And, finally, the words and phrases pertaining to Grendel's pool cannot properly be regarded as referring to the sea, even if the pool may be rather a deep seagorge or a land-locked arm of the sea (connected by an underground channel) than an inland pool, the basin of a waterfall. One of the four phrases and eight of the nine simple nouns do elsewhere in the poem refer to the sea; but here they denote and describe the pool and its waters, precisely as do the one simple noun, one compound, and one phrase which this poet uses only of the pool[6] (although other poets use them of the sea) and the four compound nouns and two phrases which, occurring in extant poetry only in these passages, never in any context refer to the sea.[7] These words and phrases constitute a group unto themselves: they merit analysis, for their use in these passages reveals not only much about their meanings but also more than many a theoretical discussion about the true nature of the pool; but they cannot justifiably be included among the terms which this poet actually applies to the sea.

Clear references to the sea itself, or to some special aspect or characteristic of it, occur in only 22 sections of the poem. There are 85 in all, of which over half, 48, are concentrated in 4 passages totaling 164 lines. Of the remaining 37, 15 occur in groups of 2 or 3, structurally connected, and 22 are scattered, isolated.

A few of the isolated instances are very general in their reference, denoting "the seas" surrounding the earth or (l. 1685) known in the North:

> *sǽ* in the construction *be sǽm twéonum*, four times (ll. 858, 1297, 1685, 1956)

Others refer to the known sea in a general way, every one used in a prepositional phrase meaning "over the sea," "on" or "to the sea," the context lending nothing to the meaning of the locutions, nor, apparently, demanding one rather than another:

> *sealt wæter* (l. 1989)
> *ýða ful* (l. 1208) [*][8]
> *wæteres hrycg* (l. 471)
> *fealu flód* (l. 1950) in the Módþrýðo-passage, with reference to the sea she crossed on her voyage from her father's home to Offa's court; the entire phrase is probably purely conventional
> *sǽ* (l. 318) in the Danish coastguard's statement to Béowulf: *Ic tó sǽ wille*
> *holm* (l. 2362) in the same sense, with *tó*; (l. 632) with *on*
> *geofon* (l. 1394) in the phrase *on gyfenes grund*

The majority of the isolated references, however—although

likewise all, with one exception, in prepositional phrases, for the most part with *ofer*—refer directly not to the sea itself, but to one aspect or one region or one characteristic of the sea. To be sure, two or three mean little more than "sea," and might well be included with the preceding group were it not that their referent is clearly a single distinguishing characteristic rather than the sea as a whole and in general; the greater number convey a particular notion which is specially suited to the context:

> *hronrád* (l. 10) refers to the expanse of the ocean around which sit the peoples who are forced to pay tribute to Scyld; emphasizes the extent of his dominion.[9]
>
> *geofenes begang* (l. 362) "the expanse of the ocean" [*]; in the construction *feorran cumene//ofer geofenes begang/Géata léode*; emphasizes the distance the Geats have traveled over the water.
>
> *flóda begang* (l. 1826) "the expanse of the flowing seas" [*]; likewise refers to and emphasizes the expanse of water between the lands of the Geats and the Danes.
>
> *sioleða bigong* (l. 2367) exact meaning not known [*]; not in a phrase, but the object of the verb *oferswam*; refers to the expanse of water over which Béowulf swam to return home from Frisia; emphasizes the distance, and his prowess.
>
> *seglrád* (l. 1429) [*] occurs in one of the pool contexts, but refers to that part of the ocean to which the nickers go to carry out their depredations, the ship-lanes.[9]
>
> *lagustréamas* (l. 297) refers to the ocean-currents to be followed by Béowulf's ship on its homeward voyage; points back to the *lagustrǽt* of l. 239.
>
> *ýða* (l. 421), as elsewhere in the poem, denotes the waves; nothing in the context demands that the word be taken as synecdoche, the actual referent being the sea.
>
> *ýða gewealc* (l. 464) "the rolling of the waves"; conveys much the same image as the *wæteres hrycg* of l. 471 and thus the approximate meaning is "sea"; the actual referent, however, is the undulating motion of the waves.
>
> *sǽwylmas* (l. 393) "the surges of the sea" [*]; much the same sense as in *ýða gewealc*, but the reference is to the waves themselves.
>
> *wæterýða* (l. 2242) "the waves of the sea" [*]; though occurring in isolation, the compound should be considered with the *holmwylm* and *ýðgewinn* of ll. 2410-2411, which likewise are used of the sea near which the dragon's barrow lies; in all three the emphasis is on the waves—surge and surf.

THE SYNONYMS FOR "SEA" IN *Beowulf*

In the small groups of two or three we sometimes find variation or parallelism which brings out similarities and differences in reference:

1) Danish coastguard's challenge: two words, both with *ofer* in parallel prepositional phrases:
   lagustrǽt (l. 239) [*] refers to the path, the course (in a spatial sense) followed by the ship across the water, "the water-highway."
   holmas (l. 240) "the high seas"; varies *lagustrǽt*, but refers either to the body of water or (more probably because of the plural form) to the high-rising waves of the area across which the highway lies.

2) Description of winter, Finn Episode: only one word in prepositional phrase, no variation:
   mere (l. 1130) "sea" with *on*; no special implications.
   holm (l. 1131) subject of the verbs *weallan* and *winnan*; thus refers to the sea as characterized by boiling billows, "high seas," the sea which moves violently.
   ýþa (l. 1132) "waves" which are "locked" by the icy bonds of winter.

3) Speech of Wealhþéow, but no particular context for "sea":
   sǽ (l. 1223) in its general sense of "the seas": *swá sǽ bebúgeð*
   windgeard (l. 1224) "enclosure of the winds" [*]; if in truth it is a variation of the *sǽ* of the preceding line,[10] it has the same referent.

4) Hróðgár's speech pledging peace between Danes and Geats: two terms, both with *ofer* in parallel prepositional phrases:
   ganotes bæð (l. 1861); same stretch of sea as that referred to in *geofenes begang* and *flóda begang,* but here Hróðgár does not wish to emphasize the distance, the *expanse* of water between the two peoples; rather, across the peaceful surface of the sea men may exchange gifts.
   hæf by emendation[11] (l. 1862) "seas" (pl. here); same referent as above; no certain special implications, although it may mean "high seas."[12]

5) Localization of the dragon's barrow: two words, both objects of same preposition, *néh*:
   holmwylm (l. 2410) "ocean-surge" [*]; sea near which the barrow lies; actual reference is to the surging motion of the open ocean, the swell of the sea; thus suggests that the headland juts into the ocean proper, not an inlet or arm of the sea.
   ýðgewinn (l. 2411) "strife of the waves" [*]; varies *holmwylm* but refers to the breaking of the waves against the rocky

headland; suggests the barrow is close by the coast; note difference in implications of *wæterýða* (l. 2242), which, having a wider semantic range, embraces both *holmwylm* and *ýðgewinn* but does not convey the same images.

6) Béowulf's last words, requesting construction of his burial mound: two words, not structurally connected but associated in the same context, both in prepositional phrases but both in the genitive in subsidiary position:

brim[es] (l. 2803) in *æt brimes nosan*; refers to the sea into which the promontory projects; context indicates it is the ocean proper.

flód[a] (l. 2808) in *ofer flóda genipu*; not the genitive phrase equivalent to a compound, but either of the type of *flódes æht* (l. 42), *ýþa ðrym* (l. 1918) or that type represented by Kock's formula, "Concrete genitive+abstract noun=adjective+concrete noun"[13]—i.e., "the misty [or dark?] tides"; refers to the tides and ocean-currents, which carry ships across the sea (*brim*) and toward the coasts.

7) Disposal of the dragon's body: two words, both as subjects of verbs of motion in parallel constructions:

wég (l. 3132) with *niman*; refers to the wave, the swell, which, rising high and seemingly reaching up, receives the falling body.

flód (l. 3134) with *fæðmian*; refers to the horizontally moving water, the tide, which encircles the body.

It is in the four extended passages, in which five or more words and phrases are used, however, that we are best able to perceive similarities and differences in reference—and that we should expect to find the piling up of synonyms, if such there be:

1) The burial of Scyld (ll. 28-52): six words, five of them in prepositional phrases but two genitives in a subsidiary position, only one the subject of a verb:

tó brimes faroðe "to the ocean's tide"; refers to that part of the sea which will carry the body out from the land, as Scyld had requested.

flód in *on flódes æht*; refers to the tides and currents which will take possession of the ship and carry it *far* (*feor*) out on and around the ocean.

holm as subject of *beran*; refers to the ocean which bears the ship.

gársecg with *on*; varies *holm*, but emphasizes not the movement, but the ocean vast and unknown.

[28]

THE SYNONYMS FOR "SEA" IN *Beowulf*

ýða with *ofer*; referring to the waves crossed by Scyld as a child, the word is not to be taken with the others in these lines.

2) Béowulf's voyage to the land of the Danes (ll. 198-228): six references, three in prepositional phrases, five words:

swanrád with *ofer*; refers to the sea [or its surface?] which Béowulf intends to cross; the first of the words in the passage to refer to the sea, is it, with its literal meaning of "the riding-place of the swan," deliberately selected to introduce the passage and to designate descriptively the body of water about to be crossed by *flota fámiheals fugle gelícost?*

ýða with *on*; refers to the waves on which the *flota* rests before it sails.

stréamas, as subject of *wundon*; refers to the currents eddying at the shore, apparently around the anchored boat.

sund (l. 213) varies *stréamas*, but may refer simply to the water swirling against the sand.

wǽgholm [*] with *ofer*; refers to the ocean across which the wind drives the *flota fámiheals*.

sund (l. 223) refers to water, either that of the sea which has been crossed when the seafarers sight land, or that lying off the promontory, which they cross between the time they sight the sea-cliffs (ll. 221-223) and the time they climb *on wang* (l. 225) and make fast the ship; the mysterious *eolet*[*es*] occurs in this sentence and obscures the sense.

3) The homeward voyage of the Geats (ll. 1888-1919): eight references, six in prepositional phrases, six words:

flód with *tó*; reference is not distinct, probably to the sea; seemingly same type of phrase as *tó sǽ* (l. 318), *tó holme* (l. 2362).

déop wæter in accusative after *dréfan;* refers to the deep water lying off the promontory, into which the Geats shove off; or to the sea.

ýða with *ofer*; refers to the waves over which the wind blows the *wégflota* onward.

ýða with *ofer*; refers to the waves over which the *fámigheals* floats.

brimstréamas with *ofer;* varies *ofer ýðe,* but refers to the ocean-currents; compare *lagustréamas*.

holm with *æt*; refers to the sea, where the harbor-guard is ready; general reference.

faroð with *æt*; refers to the tide where it comes in to shore and would bring the boat in, the wash at the shore.

ýða in genitive; refers to the waves at the shore whose force (*þrym*) could carry the ship out to sea again were it not well anchored when the voyage is at an end.

THE SYNONYMS FOR "SEA" IN *Beowulf*

4) The swimming-match with Breca (ll. 506-581), in which we should distinguish between Unferð's account (ll. 506-528) and Béowulf's (ll. 530-581) because the difference in the speaker's point of view toward the events could be reflected in the words he uses to describe those events: twenty-eight references, only twelve in prepositional phrases, sixteen words:

In Unferð's account, twelve references, eleven words:

síd sǽ with *on*; refers to the *wide* sea (i.e., the open ocean) in which the two boys competed.

wada the waters of this sea.

déop wæter with *on*; refers to the sea; emphasizes the depths in which the boys risked their lives.

sund with *on*; refers to the water in which they swam (as contrasted with *sund* with *ymb*, l. 507, and *æt*, l. 517, referring to their swimming in this water).

éagorstréam in accusative after *þehton;* refers to the ocean-current they followed (as ships follow the currents).

merestrǽta in accusative after *mǽton,* which varies *þehton;* parallel to *éagorstréam*; refers to the "sea-streets" the swimmers "measured" as riders "measure" the roads on land.

gársecg with *ofer*; parallel to the two preceding; refers to the ocean over which the boys glided, through which the *éagorstréam* flows and over which the *merestrǽta* lie; compare *lagustrǽt-holmas* (ll. 239-240).

geofon subject of *wéol*; refers to the ocean around them, presumably.

ýþa the waves produced by the surging of the *geofon*.

wylm MS reading, according to which it would vary *geofon* and refer to the sea as characterized by the surges of winter; editors emend to *wylmum* or *wylme*,[14] making it vary *ýþum* and thus refer to the billows with which the *geofon* surges.

wæter in *on wæteres ǽht*; refers to the water in which the boys remained for seven nights; compare *on flódes ǽht* (1. 42).

holm subject of *ætbær*; refers to the ocean which by its motion carried Breca up on land.

In Béowulf's account, sixteen references, twelve words. He repeats six of Unferð's words and in the same senses:

sund in the same construction *wit* [for *git*] *on sund reon*;

ýða once with *on*; once as subject of *wǽron*;

gársecg in the context in which Unferð uses *déop wæter*;

although three are used with verbs, adjectives, or variations that bring out their meanings more sharply:

sǽ once with *on;* but once as the subject of *oþbær* and varied by *flód* and *wadu weallendu*;

wada (twice) with *weallende*; once varying *flód*, subject of *tódráf;* once varying *sǽ*, subject of *oþbær;* refers to the waters of the ocean, specifically characterized by their surging motion;

holm with *on;* varies *flódýþa*.

The words Unferð does not use all occur in Béowulf's addition to the story:

flódýþa (*) refers to the rolling waves of the high seas in which Breca could not swim far from Béowulf; varied by *on holme*, it denotes a distinguishing attribute of the *holm*.

flód as subject of *tódráf* refers to the current, the whole horizontal movement of the sea, which drove the two boys apart at last; varied by *wado weallende*; standing in the same immediate context with *sǽ* (l. 544), but not varying it, these two terms (ll. 545, 546) denote—and contrast—the two characteristic movements of the sea; compare ll. 579-581, where they do vary *sǽ*.

flód (l. 580) as variation of *sǽ* subject of *oþbær;* itself in the construction *flód æfter faroðe*, it probably refers to the flowing movement of the sea, "the flow with the tide" on to shore (*on Finna land*).

ford in *ymb brontne ford*; refers to the part of the sea traversed by seafarers and infested by nickers—nine of which will infest it no more.

brimu as subject of *swaþredon;* refers to the billows which prevented Béowulf's seeing the sea-nesses.

égstréamas with *on*; refers to the ocean-currents on which Béowulf has made his wearying journey; compare *lagustréamas*.

This survey of the actual references in the poem to the sea and its characteristics and parts, compressed though it is by the exigencies of space, reveals several striking facts. First, the total number of terms in this sea-vocabulary is less than is generally supposed: 16 simple nouns, 17 compounds, and 7 genitive phrases.[15] Secondly, of these 40 words and phrases, 5 of the simple nouns account for nearly 59 per cent of the total references to the sea in the poem. *Ýð* occurs 15 times—10 in the simplex, 3 in compounds, 2 in genitive phrases; *sǽ*, 10 times—9 in simplex, 1 in compound; *holm*, 10 times—8 in simplex, 2 in compounds; *flód*, 9 times—7 in simplex, 1 in compound, 1 in genitive phrase;

wæter, 6 times—4 in simplex, 1 in compound, 1 in genitive phrase. Furthermore, as elements in compounds these 5 words occur only in those recorded from no other extant text. Third, only 7 of the 17 compounds (of which *gársecg* alone occurs more than once and 9 are found nowhere else[16]) and one of the 7 phrases (none of them occurring more than once and 4 in this poem alone[17]) stand as or with variation—a fact not wholly consistent with the view that many of these compounds and phrases owe their selection, even existence, in no small part to the demands of the stylistic device of variation. And finally, whatever later or lesser poets may do, this poet does not use all of the 40 terms as synonyms, with the general sense of "sea."

By "synonyms" I mean alternative words and locutions which have the same (or a sufficiently similar) referent; although, themselves having different semantic ranges, they may express different subjective apprehensions of the referent, different attitudes toward it, and thus, within the limits set by the context, emphasize different aspects of it. According to this definition, it does not follow that all terms *pertaining to* the sea "mean 'sea.'" The referent of *ýð* as the *Beowulf* poet (as distinct from a hypothetical "*the* Anglo-Saxon poet") uses it is the wave, the referent of *sǽ* is the sea; hence *ýð means* "wave" (in the plural "waves"), *sǽ means* "sea," and the two cannot properly be said to be synonyms.

On the basis of their actual meanings, as they are used in context by the poet, we may distinguish in the sea-vocabulary of *Beowulf* several groups of synonyms. The distinctions between the groups are indicated by the differences in reference, and thus in meaning, between the five simple words which occur most frequently. *Wæter* has a general meaning of "water," and this is its usual meaning in the poem : in one of the eighteen occurrences of the simplex (l. 516) it stands without qualification with reference to the water of the sea, but it means "water," not "sea"; when it is limited by an adjective, it in combination with the adjective means "sea" and is a synonym of *sǽ*—that is, *déop wæter* and *sealt wæter* are synonyms of *sǽ*, but *wæter* alone is not. *Sǽ* has a general meaning of "the seas," and a particular meaning of "the sea" known to and traveled by seafarers. *Holm* refers to the sea in one of its particular aspects. Cognate with OS *holm* "hill," ON *holmr* "islet" and *holmi* "rising ground," and related to Latin *celsus* "high," *collis* "hill,"[18] it would appear to characterize the ocean in terms of its distinctive undulating vertical motion— the *swell* of the open sea. It seems to mean what we mean in NE both when we speak of "the high seas"—that is, the ocean proper, the open sea, not near the coasts—and when we say that "the sea is running high."[19] It occurs but three times with or as variation: it is varied by *gársecg* (ll. 48-49), which always refers to the ocean proper, the open sea, but *holm* as subject of the verb *beran* emphasizes the motion of the ocean as *gársecg* in a prepositional phrase does not; it serves as variation for *flódýþum* (ll. 542-543), the billows that characterize the *holm* but are not identical with it; and—in the plural—for *lagustrǽt* in a context in which *holmas* might mean "swells" or might mean the open sea characterized by the swells (ll. 237-240): "who come bringing the high ship over the water-highway, hither across the high seas." The verbs of which *holm* is subject suggest the motion of the sea: *beran* (l. 48), *ǽtberan* (l. 519), *weallan* (l. 1131), *winnan* (l. 1132). The referent of *holm*, in the singular at least, is the sea itself, however, not the swells; thus in the singular the word is a synonym of *sǽ*, in the plural possibly of *ýð*. *Flód* refers to the characteristic horizontal motion of the sea, the "tide" and the periodic tidal currents, sometimes also the ocean currents and the constant perceptible horizontal *flow*. But in contradistinction to *holm*, *flód* refers directly to the motion of the sea, not to the sea itself, and thus it is not, in the great majority of its occurrences, a synonym of *sǽ,* only once, in the prepositional phrase *tó flóde* (l. 1888), does it probably, and in *ofer fealone flód* (l. 1950) possibly, refer rather to the sea than to tide or current, and thus serve as a synonym of *sǽ.*

Others of the sea-terms denote or emphasize other aspects or characteristics of the sea. *Brim* refers to the sea as characterized by foamy waves, the white-capped billows and rollers of the open sea, the breakers crashing against the rocks of the headland, the surf at the shore; but in one passage it occurs in the plural with reference to the billows themselves, and hence here (l. 570) it is a synonym of *ýð* rather than of *sǽ. Wylm* expresses the surging and the boiling of the sea. We cannot be certain whether in *Beowulf* the simple noun refers to the sea as characterized by this movement, or to the movement itself, for in the sole passage in which it pertains to the sea it stands in the MS as variation for *geofon,* but on metrical grounds is customarily emended into variation (and synonym) for *ýþum* (ll. 515-516). The probability is that the word refers to the movement itself, for in other applications in the poem it refers to the *gushing* of the burn (l. 2546), the *surging* of the water of the Flood (l. 1693), the *surgings* of the [blood of the] heart (l. 2507), and—most vividly, with the verb not only adding to the sense of movement but also revealing the nature of the movement—the *swelling rise* of death in the image *déaðes wylm // hrán æt heortan* (ll. 2269-2270). In the plural it would probably, like *brim* and possibly *holm,* refer to the product of the movement, the waves; it does in the compound *sǽwylmas* (l. 393). *Faroð* refers to the horizontal movement of the water of the sea, but is more limited in its referential range than is *flód*: it refers to the tide and the tidal currents near or at the shore-line. *Sund* refers to the water of the sea, once (l. 213) "water" without qualification, but in the other instances

THE SYNONYMS FOR "SEA" IN Beowulf

once probably and twice quite clearly *deep* water. Since this is undeniably the word which in NE means "sound," a narrow channel between two bodies of water or between the mainland and one or more islands, and since it seems to be the same word as that which in ON as well as OE means "swimming," it is sometimes explained as meaning, or having meant at an early stage of its semantic development, literally "water one can swim across."[20] But in *Beowulf* there is no suggestion of this element of "narrowness" : the word is used twice of the water which Béowulf crosses on his voyage from the land of the Geats to Heorot, although, to be sure, once it is the water lapping on the Geatish shore;[21] and twice of the water in which Béowulf and Breca swim, the *déop wæter* (l. 509), the *gársecg* (l. 515, l. 537), the *holm* (l. 543)—that is, the water of the deep ocean. As an element in the compounds *sundgerd* (*sundgyrd*) "sounding pole," *sundline* "sounding lead," *sund-* rather implies depth than width. In l. 213 the referent is the water; in the other three instances it may be either deep water or the sea as characterized by its depth. *Wæd* also is used with reference to the waters in which Béowulf and Breca swim: it occurs three times, twice qualified by *weallende* and once with possibly the same referent as *déop wæter* (ll. 508-510). The expanse of the sea, its surface, and special areas and regions of it are expressed only by bipartite locutions—simple nouns with adjectives, compounds, and genitive phrases,—which afford the two formal elements necessary to designate the two notions involved in the concept.

Thus we may distinguish seven groups of synonyms in the sea-vocabulary of *Beowulf*:

1) referent: *the sea*, in general or in one of its aspects: seventeen words and phrases[22]
    A. Synonyms for "sea" and normally for each other: *sǽ, mere, déop wæter, sealt wæter, hæf, geofon, windgeard, ýða ful, wæteres hrycg*.

B. Synonyms for "sea," but not all for each other: *gársecg, holm, wǽgholm, brim, ganotes bæð, swanrád, sund* (?), *flód*(?).
2) referent: *the water* of the sea: three words: *wæter, sund, wadu.*
3) referent: *the horizontal movement* of the sea, "tide" and "current": seven words, not all synonyms of each other: *flód, faroð, stréamas, brimstréamas, éagorstréam, égstréamas, lagustréamas.*
4) referent: *the vertical movement* of the sea, the "surge": four words and phrases: *wǽg, holmwylm, wylm* (?), *ýða gewealc.*
5) referent: *the waves*: seven words: *ýða, flódýþa, wæterýða, brimu, sǽwylmas, wylmas* (?), *holmas*(?).
6) referent: *the expanse* of the sea: four words and phrases: *hronrád, flóda begang, geofenes begang, sioleða bigong.*
7) referent: *a special region* of the sea: two locutions (both of which occur only in *Beowulf*): *bront ford, seglrád.*

The remaining three words, two of which (*lagustrǽt* and *ýðgewinn*) occur only in this poem, are peculiarly suited to their contexts and find no synonyms in the poem.

We may conclude that it is altogether true that "the large part which the sea played in the life of the Beowulfian peoples, finds expression in an astonishing wealth of terms applied to it,"[28] but that this wealth consisted not in sheer numbers of words and locutions all with the same meaning, but rather in the variety of terms and their appropriateness to the varied aspects and characteristics of the sea itself.

We turn now to consideration of the second problem, the extent to which this sea-vocabulary is figurative. Actually, we are concerned with but one figure: the metaphor. Synecdoche, usually considered ubiquitous throughout the poem, is of little moment here, and particular instances that are important to this discussion are better considered in connection with the locutions in which they are found. The other figures concern the present discussion not at all. The metaphor, on the other hand, is of peculiar importance in the diction and style of Old English poetry; and inadequate understanding both of the metaphors themselves and of what we mean by the term can lead (and too often has led) to false and largely subjective judgments concerning this diction.[24]

By "metaphor" in this context I mean that figure of speech which represents an intentional transfer, for purposes of æsthetic enhancement, of a word or locution from the referent it traditionally may designate to a new referent having no essential identity with the primary referent but belonging to another sphere of experience. The word or locution used metaphorically, like the "plain" designation from which it is to be distinguished, expresses a meaning which lies within its traditional semantic range; but unlike the "plain" designation, it designates a referent which lies outside its traditional referential range. The ensuing tension between the primary meaning and the actual reference is always present in the "live" metaphor.

In identifying the metaphors in *Beowulf* we are hampered by the fact that as yet we do not know as much as we should about the semantic range of many words, especially the more common ones, in the ordinary nonpoetic language of the day. Consequently, when in a passage of poetry we come upon a sense which seems to us unusual, we cannot always be certain whether an element within the traditional semantic range of the word has for the momentary context been shifted to the central position from the peripheral position it occupies in other (most) contexts, or whether an actual transfer from one referent to another has taken place. This disadvantage is especially acute when we are dealing with the compounds and genitive phrases, for as a whole they have never received adequate semantic analysis. With inadequate knowledge of the meanings of their component parts, we are likely to find metaphors where none exist. The compounds in *-lád* afford an excellent example. In nearly all the earlier studies of the sea-vocabulary, these are listed as synonyms for "sea," with -*lád* bearing the sense of "path," "*Weg*," *via;* thus interpreted, they would be metaphors. Now, however, it has been recognized that in *Beowulf* they do not refer to the sea and that in this poem -*lád* has its primary meaning of "journey";[25] hence no metaphor is involved.

None of the simple nouns pertaining to the sea in *Beowulf* is used metaphorically. All are simple appellatives, literal designations of their referents. Shift there is in the application of *flód* (and *sund*?) to the sea, but it is not intentional transfer. *Flód* seems to be on its way to a change of meaning, but, so far as *Beowulf* would indicate, has not yet passed through it; we observed that it occurs with reference to the sea only in two prepositional phrases, in both of which it could mean "tide" although it probably means "sea," and I should guess that the change involved is what Stern calls "permutation."[26] The history of this word as well as that of *sund* needs further investigation. Neither is metaphor involved in the use of the plurals *brimu* and -*wylmas* (and *holmas*?) to denote a distinguishing characteristic of the referent of the singulars. Of all the simple nouns, *ford* alone seems to be used in a strikingly unusual sense; indeed, Klaeber marks it with a double dagger to indicate that this sense is found only in this one passage in *Beowulf*. Qualified by *bront,* which must be taken together with it, it does seem to be metaphorical in that "sea" would seem to be out of the traditional referential range of *ford* and in that an additional tension seems to exist in the relation between the two elements, *ford* and *bront*. But whereas a ford is ordinarily a place where water may be crossed by wading, and thus "by wading" is a central element of the usual meaning of the word, the notion of "going" or "crossing" is likewise an element within its semantic range—and an important one, since the noun is associated with the verb *faran*. Thus with a shift in emphasis from one element of meaning to another, a shift that puts "by wading" on the periphery rather than in a central position, the word means simply "a place where water may be crossed," "fahrbare, passierbare Stelle," "fahrbare Stelle im Wasser."[27] *Bront ford* means "a deep crossing," "deep passage," with reference to the sea "a place where ships may pass"; this is clearly the meaning in the context in which the locution occurs : Béowulf has killed the nickers, "so that never afterwards did they hinder the journey of the sea-travellers about the deep passage." *Bront ford* designates that region of the sea through which the ships pass, and thus is a synonym of *seglrád*.[28]

Like the simple nouns, the majority of the compounds and genitive phrases are literal in their reference, only one-fourth of the total number involving actual intentional transfers. The problem of analysis is more complicated, however, for we have to consider not merely the meanings of the component parts, but also the relations between the two elements and between the parts and the whole. All—the meaning of each of the parts, the relation between them, the relation between them and the whole, the meaning of the whole— may be strictly literal. On the other hand, at least one, possibly both, of the elements of the compound or phrase may be a metaphor; and consequently in the relation between the two elements, and in some instances in the relation between the sum of the parts and the whole, will exist that tension between primary meaning and actual reference which is the essence of metaphor. Again, on the basis of the relation between the parts and the whole we distinguish two principal types: the periphrasis and the direct bipartite designation. In this latter type the whole is exactly the number of the parts, meaning no more than the two parts together mean; the formula is 1+2=1+2. In the periphrasis the whole is the total of the parts, its referent a third notion standing outside of the compound or phrase but defined or described by the two elements together; the formula is

THE SYNONYMS FOR "SEA" IN *Beowulf*

1+2=3. Within these major groups are several classes : the direct bipartite designations consist of literal designating compounds and phrases, literal descriptive compounds, and metaphorical compounds; the periphrases are the literal defining periphrasis and the metaphorical.

Exactly half of the compounds and genitive phrases pertaining to the sea are bipartite appellatives, like the simple nouns literal designations of their referents: *brimstréamas, éagorstréam, égstréamas, lagustréamas, flodýþa, wæterýða, holmwylm, sǽwylmas, flóda begang, geofenes begang,* and *ýða gewealc.* Presumably, *sioleða bigong* belongs in this class, although since we do not know what *sioloð* means we are unable to classify it with certainty. No one of these is a synonym for "sea," and therefore none is synecdochic; all refer to some special aspect or characteristic of the sea, none to the sea as characterized by these aspects or characteristics. All are to be taken literally in their contexts; and whether like *ýða gewealc, geofenes begang,* and *wæterýða* they stand in isolation, or like *holmwylm* and *flódýþa* with variation, their meaning is clear in itself. Bipartite in construction, all are bipartite in meaning: in *brimstréamas*, for example, *brim-* serves the double purpose of indicating that these are the ocean-currents over which the boat is now sailing, as distinct from the shore-currents eddying around it as it lay at anchor, and of suggesting the white-capped billows over which the foamy-necked floater is now skimming; *flódýþa* emphasizes, as *ýþa* alone could not, the constant rolling of the waves.

Wægholm is a literal descriptive compound, both designating the ocean by *-holm* and describing it by *wǽg-*. Occurring only once, the word is perfectly suited to its context. The same wind that is driving the *flota fámiheals fugle gelícost* is blowing up the waves on the ocean. Imagery is here, but not necessarily metaphor. I should also place in this class the long-debated *gársecg*.

[40]

Kemp Malone has identified the first element with the *gár* of *Genesis* 316, which he takes to mean "storm."[29] The second element he takes as *secg* "warrior"; and he concludes: "the sea may perfectly well be thought of as a warrior whose weapon is the storm. And *gársecg*, so taken, exemplifies a familiar method of formation: compare *æscwiga, sweordfreca*, and the like, where the first element is a weapon name, the second a word meaning 'warrior.'"[30] His interpretation of *gár* must be accepted, of that there can be no doubt. But compounds like *æscwiga* and *sweordfreca* are not analogous to *gársecg*: they are literal designating compounds, the whole meaning no more than the two parts together mean, the referent being the warrior; *gársecg* in the sense of "warrior with a storm=ocean" would be a doubly metaphorical periphrasis, expressing a third notion standing outside the compound itself. The disparity is so great as to be dangerous to discount if we can find another reasonable explanation of *gársecg*. The simplex *segg* (Corpus, S85: *seeg vel mare*) occurs in the Épinal, Erfurt, and Corpus Glossaries (as well as Wright-Wülcker's Glossary VIII,[31] which in this section seems related to these three) as a gloss for *salum*. Malone believes this to be "presumably a derivative of *garsecg* by abbreviation." On the other hand, the Corpus Glossary also preserves as a gloss for *salum* the word *hæf*, which in literary texts is found only in *Beowulf*. It is reasonable to assume that even as the first element of *gársecg* is a noun recorded in the simplex only in the early poem *Genesis*, so is the second a noun recorded in the simplex only in glossaries from the seventh and eighth centuries, and that the compound was constructed at an early date from these two simple nouns, both of which seem since to have disappeared from the written language. This explanation would better account for the occurrence of *gársecg* in glossaries, as well as in Ælfred's *Orosius*, as a gloss for *Oceanus* than will the long-held theory that it is an elaborate metaphorical periphrasis that somehow strayed into the common speech at an early date. *Gársecg* would be like *wǽgholm,* a literal descriptive compound. It would mean "the open sea characterized by storms,"[32] " the stormy ocean," Oceanus; it would express the same aspect of the sea as does the unique *windgeard* "the enclosure of the winds." In *Beowulf* it never occurs in isolation, where the reference could be to the sea in general, but only in contexts where it clearly refers to the open ocean.

The compounds *hronrád, seglrád,* and *swanrád* and the phrase *ganotes bæð,* as well as *bront ford,* are literal defining periphrases. As I have shown elsewhere,[33] *rád* did not mean "road" in OE, and thus no metaphor is involved in its use in compounds pertaining to the sea. All define, in literal terms, the sea or one region of the sea as an area in which the whale, the ship, or the swan "rides [the waves]." There is synecdoche in the use of *segl-* for "ship," but no metaphor in any of the three. All occur in isolation, although *swanrád* is followed some ten lines later by a descriptive passage, and may justifiably be regarded as belonging to that passage. Similarly, *ganotes bæð* defines the surface of the sea as the area, or, possibly, the water of the sea as the liquid, in which the gannet dips or "bathes"; either sense would be satisfactory in the context in which the locution occurs. *Bæð* occurs infrequently in OE, but with such diversity of reference that it requires further investigation. However, in the application of the locution to the actual referent is no transfer, intentional or unintentional, from a referent belonging in another sphere of experience; for it is not *bæð* that refers to the sea, but *bæð* in terms of and as limited by *ganot-*. This is one important meaning of the formula $1+2=3$. Within itself the phrase is literal, for the gannet is a sea-bird which does, literally, "bathe" in the sea, just as the whale is a sea-animal which does literally roll and sway and travel and generally "ride" in the sea. The distinction between locutions like these and one like *ýða ful* is fundamental: for not only can the sea be conceived of as a "cup of waves" only through a transfer, intentional obviously, from one referent to another which is not, even for the moment, *essentially* identical; but, since wave and cup do not belong in the same sphere of experience, or even related spheres, since between them exists or can be established no matter-of-fact relation, the combination of the two into a single unit of reference sets up a discord that can be reconciled only by means of a subsidiary image, a second metaphor.

Ýða ful, wæteres hrycg, and *windgeard* are metaphorical periphrases. They stand in isolation, and their reference is to the sea in general. The first element of each is synecdochic or metonymic in that it names one attribute or one accompanying circumstance of the referent of the whole; but the locution as a whole neither directly designates nor literally describes or defines its referent. These three—and only these three—are genuine metaphorical synonyms for "sea."

Metaphorical, but of quite another order, are *lagustrǽt, merestrǽt,* and *ýðgewinn*. These, the metaphorical compounds, are, like the literal designating compounds and phrases, bipartite in meaning as well as in structure. They differ from the bipartite appellatives only in that their second element is a metaphor: compare *lagustrǽt* and *lagustréamas*. None of these refers to the sea; each has its own special meaning in the context in which it occurs: these are the three compounds for which we could find no synonyms in the poem. For despite their superficial identity out of context, *lagustrǽt* and *merestrǽt* are not synonyms. *Lagustrǽt* in its context refers to the "water-highway" *ofer holmas* across which Béowulf has brought his ship to the Danish coast. *Merestrǽt* is altogether different—and individual— in its reference: together with the verb of which it is the object it has been transferred, with the substitution of *mere-* for *fealu* or a similar word, to the sea-context of the swimming match from the land-contexts in which it traditionally belongs: e.g., *fealwe strǽte // méarum mǽton* (ll. 916-917); *foldweg mǽton, // cúþe strǽte* (ll. 1633-1634). Likewise, *ýðgewinn* is peculiarly suited to its context: in this context (l. 2412) it is a variation of *holmwylm*, but not a synonym, for it designates the pounding of the waves against the headland, "the strife *of* the waves"; in the sole other extant context in which it occurs (l. 1434) it means "struggle *against* the waves," that is, "swimming."

In conclusion, we must say that the metaphorical content in the sea-vocabulary of *Beowulf* is negligible. "Pictorial" many of the terms are, but only six of the forty words and phrases actually used with reference to the sea or to some characteristic or special aspect of it are or contain metaphors; and of these only three may properly be called "metaphorical terms for the sea." In depicting the sea this poet is no artificer mechanically piling up synonyms and conventional metaphors, but an artist who knows how to use a variety of words and phrases in their literal senses to convey the effect he desires.

References

1. I do not include compounds and phrases in which words from the sea-vocabulary are used as elements of composition but which actually refer to voyage, ship, seafarer, shore, cliffs, etc.

2. Klaeber in his Glossary gives the sense "sea" for only a little over two-thirds of the total number; but cf. Albert H. Tolman, "The Style of Anglo-Saxon Poetry," *PMLA*, III (1887), 26: "I find forty-two simple and compound nouns in 'Beowulf' which mean *ocean*, and ten nouns + genitives." The translators treat the terms as though they were readily interchangeable; compare the renderings of the words and phrases in ll. 28-52 and 198-228 appearing in five of the most widely circulated translations, those of Gummere, Kennedy, Whiting, Spaeth, and Leonard: *tó brimes faroðe*—ocean's billow—shore of the ocean—shore of the sea—brink of the sea—sea-tides; *flód*—flood—unknown deep—water—waves—floods; *ýða*—seas—sea—waves—billows—wave; *holm*—billows—wave—sea—surges—billows; *gársecg*—ocean—trackless deep—ocean— — — deep: *swanrád*—swan-road—swan-road—swan-road—swan-road—swan-road; *ýða*— —waves—waves—water— ———; *stréamas*—waves—billows—currents—tide—breakers; *sund*—sea—sea—water—sea—[tide?]; *wǽgholm*—waters—breaking billows—sea—waves—waves of the waters; *sund*—hawn—sea—sea—harbor—ocean.

[44]

THE SYNONYMS FOR "SEA" IN *Beowulf*

3. Cf. Karl Schemann, *Die Synonyma im Béowulfsliede mit Rücksicht auf Composition und Poetik des Gedichtes*, Diss., Hagen, 1882, pp. 34 ff., 92 ff.; Hans Merbach, *Das Meer in der Dichtung der Angelsachsen*, Diss., Breslau, 1884; Tolman, *op. cit.*, pp. 26 f.; Edmund Erlemann, *Das landschaftliche Auge der angelsächsischen Dichter*, Diss., Berlin, 1902, pp. 26 ff.; Stopford A. Brooke, *The History of Early English Literature*, New York, 1914, pp. 162 ff.; Henry Cecil Wyld, "Diction and Imagery in Anglo-Saxon Poetry," *Essays and Studies by Members of the English Association*, XI (1925), 58 ff.; Robert Ashton Kissack, Jr., "The Sea in Anglo-Saxon and Middle English Poetry," *Washington University Studies*, XIII (1926), 371 ff.; Anne Treneer, *The Sea in English Literature from Beowulf to Donne*, London, 1926, pp. 3 ff. [analysis by passages rather than lists]; Helen Thérèse McMillan Buckhurst, "Terms and Phrases for the Sea in Old English Poetry," *Studies in English Philology. A Miscellany in Honor of Frederick Klaeber*, Minneapolis, 1929, pp. 103 ff.; Hertha Marquardt, *Die altenglischen Kenningar. Ein Beitrag zur Stilkunde altgermanischer Dichtung*, Halle, 1938, pp. 164 ff., and *passim* [she does sometimes analyze locutions in context].

4. On this distinction between lexical and actual meaning, see Gustaf Stern, "Meaning and Change of Meaning," *Göteborgs Högskolas Årsskrift*, XXXVIII:1 (1932), 68 ff.

5. *Beowulf and the Fight at Finnsburg*, ed. Fr. Klaeber, 3 ed., Boston, 1936.

6. *lagu, fyrgenstréam, ýða geswing*.

7. *brimwylm, meregrund, sundgebland, ýðgeblond; ýða gewin, holma geþring*.

8. The asterisk here and hereafter is equivalent to Klaeber's double dagger, indicating that the word has been preserved only in *Beowulf*.

9. See my article, "The Old English Nominal Compounds in *-rád*," *PMLA*, LXVII (June, 1952), 538 ff.

10. See Klaeber's note to the line.

11. MS reads *heafu*, but see Klaeber's note. *Hæb* occurs in the Corpus Glossary (S 59; ed. W. M. Lindsay, Cambridge, 1921, p. 157) as a gloss for *salum*.

12. See H. S. Falk and Alf Torp, *Norwegisch-Dänisches etymologisches Wörterbuch*, Heidelberg, 1910, I, 385 f.; F. Holthausen, *Altenglisches etymologisches Wörterbuch*, Heidelberg, 1934, p. 144.

13. So Marquardt, *op. cit.*, p. 134.

14. See Johannes Hoops, *Kommentar zum Beowulf*, Heidelberg, 1932, p. 79.

15. Cf., e.g., Tolman's 42 nouns and 10 phrases, *op. cit.*, pp. 26 f.; Schemann's 40 nouns and 12 phrases, *op. cit.*, pp. 34 ff.; Kissack's partial list of 45 terms, which omits 11 of mine, *op. cit.*, p. 373.

16. *flódýpa, holmwylm, lagustrǽt, sǽwylmas, seglrád, wǽgholm, wæterýða, windgeard, ýðgewinn*.

17. *ýða ful, flóda begang, geofenes begang, sioleða bigong*. Phrases in *begang* occur elsewhere, but the limiting words are different.

18. Holthausen, *op. cit.*, p. 169.

19. Wyld, *op. cit.*, p. 55, thinks it "probably originally meant 'the high, lofty sea; the billowy, wave-broken sea'; it may also have referred to the 'crest' or 'summit' of a wave"; Brooke, *op. cit.*, p. 163, sees in it "the up-mounding of the Ocean .... Hence it came to mean the high waves, each wave like a rounded height ...."

20. E.g., by Brooke, *op. cit.*, p. 164; Buckhurst, *op. cit.*, p. 106.

21. The parallels in the descriptions of the two voyages are rather remarkable, as is readily apparent if we read the words in the order of their occurrence, remembering that the second group reverses the order of the first. Most obvious is the parallel (and variation) in the *wǽgholm* on which the *wind* impels the *flota fámíheals* : the *ýða* over which the *wind* impels the *wégflota*; the *ýða* on which the *fámigheals fléat*; the *brimstréamas*. Then, is the *sund* mentioned at the end of the first passage the *déop wæter* at the beginning of the second?

[45]

22. Some of the simple nouns appear more than once in the following lists; consequently, the total number of entries here is greater than the total number of words and phrases in the sea-vocabulary.

23. Klaeber, *Beowulf*, pp. lix f.

24. For example, Wyld, *op. cit.*, p. 58, finds such compounds and phrases as *wǽgholm* and *ýða gewealc* "impressive by reason of their truth and beauty" and *swanrád, hronrád, ganotes bæd,* and *ýða ful* "no more vital" than those phrases of the eighteenth century which "express no emotion, . . . add nothing to our stock of vivid and beautiful images, . . . reveal no justness of observation or insight. . .do not strike the imagination and set the mind 'voyaging on strange seas of thought' . . . contain, indeed, nothing of the essence of true poetry." Kissack, *loc. cit.*, on the contrary, finds in the same *swanrád, hronrád,* and *ganotes bæð* "a decidedly strong feeling expressed. . .; and it is a highly enthusiastic and poetic feeling of pleasure."

25. See Marquardt, *op. cit.*, pp. 171 f.

26. *Op. cit.*, pp. 351 ff.

27. Johannes Hoops, "Beowulfstudien," *Anglistische Forschungen*, LXXIV (1932), 99.

28. Furthermore, nickers are the real subject of the two passages in which the two words occur; cf. my article cited above, n. 9.

29. The interpretation "tempest" for the *gár* of Gen. 316 had been tentatively put forward by John R. Clark Hall, *A Concise Anglo-Saxon Dictionary*, 3 ed., Cambridge, 1931; a connection between *gársecg* and the *gár* of Gen. was questioningly indicated by Klaeber in his Glossary, p. 338.

30. "Old English *Gár* 'Storm,'" *English Studies*, XXVIII (1947), 42 ff.

31. Thomas Wright, *Anglo-Saxon and Old English Vocabularies*, ed. Richard Paul Wülcker, London, 1884, I, 278, 22.

32. The interpretation "das offene Meer" was proposed by F. Holthausen, "Etymologien," *Indogermanische Forschungen*, XXV (1909), 153 f., who took the element *-secg* as related to ON *saggi* "Feuchtigkeit."

33. See n. 9.

Compounds of the *Mann-skratti* Type

STEFÁN EINARSSON

Johns Hopkins University

WHEN WRITING A textbook of Icelandic, I had occasion to use a certain type of Icelandic compound word and found that it could not be matched in English, except through circumlocution. This was the compound of the type *mann-skratti* "a devil of a man."

Although this type of compound is extremely common in Icelandic, especially in the colloquial language, I could find no trace of it in Alexander Jóhannesson, *Die Komposita im Isländischen* (Reykjavík, 1929=Rit Vísindafélags Íslendinga, IV). Nor could I find it mentioned in other pertinent literature about Icelandic, and though Guðmundur Finnbogason uses one word of the type in "Bölv og ragn" (*Skírnir*, 101 [1927], 48-61) in no way does he indicate the function of this type of word as used in Icelandic cursing.

Searching for parallels in the other Scandinavian languages, I found only few and doubtful examples in Danish and in Norwegian, but a considerable number in Swedish. Faroese, the link between Icelandic and Norwegian, yielded but one certain example.

In Danish of the older period (O. Kalkar, *Ordbog til det ældre danske sprog 1300-1700*) I found, under *mand* and *pige*: *mand-helt* 'man-hero,' 'en mandig helt' (P. Clausen's translation of Snorri Sturluson's *Heimskringla*); *mand-kærling* 'en som lader sig styre af sin hustru, en fejg mand'; *mande-rad* 'et magert menneske' (cf. *ben-rad* 'skeleton').

V. Dahlerup, *Ordbog over det danske Sprog* (for modern

[47]

Danish) yielded nothing for *pige* and only *mand-fjols* 'a foolish person' and *mand-kælling* 'an effeminate man' for *mand*.

In Swedish for the older period (K. F. Söderwall, *Ordbok öfver svenska medeltidsspråket*) I found only *man-skam* 'föraktlig eller usel menniska, usling' (from *ca.* 1420 in *Bonaventuras betraktelser öfver Christi leverne*, ed. G. E. Klemming). For the modern period, however, instances abound, as a survey of *dräng* 'boy, farmhand' and *flicka* 'girl' in *Svenska Akademiens Ordbok öfver svenska språket* proves:

> *dräng-luns* 'tölpig dräng' (Strindberg).
> *dräng-slok* föraktfullt om dräng (Weste, 1807).
> *dräng-slusk* föraktligt om dräng (Envallsson, 1784).
> *flick-byting* 'liten (vild eller ostyrig) flicka' (Envallsson, 1784).
> *flick-jänta* (vardags och bygdemålsfärgat) (Berndtson, 1880).
> *flick-lunsa* (vardags) 'lunsig flicka' (Öman, 1889).
> *flick-slamsa* (vardags) ringaktande: 'yr och slamsig flicka' (Hedenstierna, 1893).
> *flick-slinka* ringaktande (Blanche, 1864).
> *flick-slyna* ringaktande (Cavallin, 1897).
> *flick-slänga* ringaktande (Wetterbergh, 1854).
> *flick-snärta* skämtsamt ringaktande (Meurman, 1846).
> *flick-stackare* (Backman, 1870).
> *flick-stumpa* smeksamt om liten flicka (Hagberg, 1849).
> *flick-tana* föraktligt om tanig flicka (Günther, 1917).
> *flick-tossa* (vardags) (Björn, 1794).
> *flick-unge* liten flicka (Björn, 1794).

Since *Svenska Akademiens Ordbok* has not been compiled as far as the word *pojke* 'boy,' I looked this word up in H. Vendell's *Ordbok över de Östsvenska dialecterna*. The result was overwhelming: *pojk-, -bissel, -divel, -gaffel, -gafs, -garp, -glaff, -glunt, -kläpp, -knubbel, -knyffel, -krällare, -pörvel, -snott, -snyffel, -vas, -vrede, -vräkling, -välpel, -vässel*—all meaning 'boy' with the added connotation of fun, endearment, scolding, pity, condescension, etc.

In spite of this striking abundance of examples E. Hellquist really does not mention this class in his discussion of word-com-

pounding (*Ordbildning*) in his *Svensk etymologisk ordbok* (Lund, 1922, p. lxii), although he does mention compounds in which the first element 'står till det senare i appositionellt förhållande, t. ex. *blomkål, drängpojke* (jfr. got. *þiu-magus* [and as he might have added: Icelandic *svein-barn*])."
I can see no reason for this omission, unless he excludes these compounds on the ground that they are not standard Swedish (*hög-svenska*) but colloquial, or unless he, like Alexander Jóhannesson, overlooks the native growth because he does not find the category treated in German works on linguistics. Indeed, I think the latter is the more reasonable explanation.[1]

For Norwegian I consulted T. Knudsen og Alf Sommerfelt, *Norsk riksmåls-ordbok* as well as Ivar Åsen, *Norsk ordbok* and Einar Haugen, *Norwegian Word Studies* (with concordances of H. Wergeland, I. Åsen, and S. Undset), but I found nothing under *mann* or *pike;* and while the word *jent-ungen* 'the little girl' may be interpreted to fit our category of compounds, it may be of the same type as Hellquist's *dräng-pojke* above. But Åsen mentions *guta(r)gnasse,* which must be a compound of our type, and Chr. Vidsteen, *Ordbog over Bygdemaalene i Söndhordland* (1901), has *mann-skræma* 'grov og barsk person,' which obviously belongs here too.

Of course, I did no more than sample the Scandinavian dictionaries at my disposal. But the sampling shows that the category is common in colloquial Swedish, and apparently very rare in colloquial Danish. If Norwegian also lags behind, it might be because of Danish influence, for the type is frequent in Old Icelandic, hence presumably at least known in Old Norwegian too.

German, on the other hand, as sampled under *Mann* in Grimm's *Wörterbuch*, yielded nothing comparable. Nearest in form were *Mannfisch* 'triton' (i.e., 'a man who is at the same time a fish'), *Mann-pferd* 'centaurus' ('man-horse'), and *Mann-thier* 'man-animal.' None of these terms has the meaning 'fish, horse, animal of a man.' The personal name *Manteuffel* (which Cleasby-Vigfússon in their *Old Icelandic Dictionary* refer to under *mann-djöfull*) seems to have originated in Pomerania (of Slavonic origin?) and may not at all be comparable to the Icelandic. But, as Professor Leo Spitzer has pointed out to me, German does seem to have at least one real parallel in *Weibs-teufel* 'a devil of a woman.'[1]

Nevertheless, the type is obviously practically nonexistent in German (which explains the silence of the German linguists). The fact that the type is virtually unknown in German, the Romance languages (according to Spitzer's information), and English (not found in H. Koziol, *Handbuch der englischen Wortbildungslehre*), has prompted linguists like Brugmann and Hirt to ignore it in their great compendia of the Indo-European languages.

But it is found in Sanskrit, as one might expect of that compound-loving language. J. S. Speijer (*Sanskrit Syntax*, 1886, pp. 163-164) classifies the type as a kind of *tatpurusha*: "The tatpurusha serves also to express comparison. Such compounds are partly adjectives, partly substantives. The former are of the type ... cloud-black... sky-blue. The latter are made up of the thing's real name + the image under which it is represented. ... The latter type is adapted to signify either praise or blame...." He goes on to remark that

> according to vernacular grammars this class of compounds is to be considered a subdivision of the *karmadhârayas*. . . . This explanation cannot be right. In fact, we have here no *karmadhârayas* but *shashthîsamâsas*. The former member is a genitive, but it does not bear everywhere the same character. Sometimes it is a partitive one, as ... *rājāpasadah* [=king-outcast] 'an outcast among kings.' ... Sometimes, too, it is a genitive of the kind, represented by our 'a jewel of a woman,' 'a hell of a fellow,' Lat. *scelus hominis*, so

COMPOUNDS OF THE Mann-skratti TYPE

gṛhabhûtih [=house-beauty] 'a beauty of a house'... bhāryācelam [=wife-slut] 'a slut of a wife.' Not rarely both acceptations [!] are alike probable, strīratnam [=woman-jewel], for instance, may be as well 'a jewel among women' as='a jewel of a woman.'

Professor P. Dumont, who called my attention to this book and helped to transcribe the Sanskrit words, prefers the translation 'a jewel among women.'

J. Wackernagel (*Altindische Grammatik*, 1905, Bd. II, 1, p. 252) describes the type—a subdivision within the great class of *Determinativ-komposita* (*Tat-purusha*)—as follows: "Klassisch häufig sind Komposita, in denen das Vorderglied die eigentliche, das Hinterglied eine bildiche Bezeichnung des auszudrückenden Begriffes gibt... z. B., *purusha-vyāghra-* 'ein Mann wie ein Tiger.'"

We are now ready to turn to the Icelandic material. In *Lexicon Poeticum* we find two words belonging to our category. One of these, *mann-baldr* 'udmærket Menneske,' 'a Balder of a man,' is from the *Tögdrápa* (1028) of Þórarinn loftunga:

Giolld hefi ek marka
malmdyns fyrir hlyn
fram fim tigu
foruist borið
þeiRa er veitti
vighagr brag
mer mordstorir
mannballdr er ek fann.

Other examples occur in the twelfth century *Þulur* (of *Manna heiti*), in Snorri Sturluson's *Háttatal* (*ca.* 1218), and in a verse of *Einarr draumr Þorsteinsson* of the thirteenth century. The second word, *mann-hundr* 'mand, der er hund, eller som en hund (skældsord), skurk,' 'a dog of a man,' is from an anonymous verse of 1234, preserved in the *Sturlunga saga*:

erv brennv menn þa
mann hunndar hia.

COMPOUNDS OF THE *Mann-skratti* TYPE

Turning to the prose dictionaries of Old Icelandic we find in Cleasby-Vigfússon:

kvenn-skinn womankind in a low sense (*Maríu saga*).
-*skratti* a bad woman (*Gísla saga*).
-*skörungur* a stately, great lady (*Njála, Dropl. saga*).
mann-baldr a great good man (*Edda*).
-*djöfull* a demon in human shape (*Fornsögur* 36); cf. Germ. *Manteuffel.*
-*fjándi* a human fiend (*Fornsögur* 36, 44, *Fornms.* II, 83).
-*fýla* a 'foul person,' rascal (*Njála* 56, *Fornsögur* 39, etc).
-*gersemi* 'a jewel of a man' (*Bisks.* I, 81, *Þiðr.* 153).
-*hundr* 'man-dog,' scoundrel (*Flatb.* I, 354, *Gísla s.,* etc.).
-*leysi* a good-for-nothing person (*Fornms.* II, 62).
-*lydda*=*mann-læra* (*Elucidarius*).
-*læra* a bad person (*Fornms.* II, 62, *Valla-Ljóts s.* 218).
-*níðingr* a 'nithing,' miscreant (*Ljósv. s.* 44. *Ólafs s. helga* 157).
-*skelmir* a rascal (*Fornaldars.* I, 330).
-*skepna* poor creature (*Rímbeygla* 360, *Fornaldars.* III, 644).
-*skratti* a wicked man.
-*skræfa* a miserable coward (*Fornms.* II, 61, 93; *Grettis s.,* etc.).
-*tetur* a 'tatter of a man,' a poor wretch.

Since Fritzner does not have *mann-skratti* and *mann-tetur* they might be Modern Icelandic words, entered by Vigfússon.

Fritzner has, in addition to the above:

mann-bikkja Skjældsord om fortagtelige Mennesker (*Postulas.* 151[81]).
-*engill* Engel i Menneskeskikkelse (*Breta s.* 27 [12[27]]).
-*fóli* tosset foragteligt Menneske (*Laxd. s.* 85 [236[32]], *Vatsd. s.* 25 [40[20]]).
-*læða*=*mann-leysi, mann-læra* (*Valla-Ljóts* s. 5[89]).

Turning now to Modern Icelandic, we print the relevant material found in Blöndal's *Íslenzk-dönsk orðabók,* marking with an asterisk those words which are found in the Old Icelandic dictionaries, and adding an English translation to such words as are also found (or found only) in G. T. Zoega's *Íslenzk-ensk orðabók.*

COMPOUNDS OF THE Mann-skratti TYPE

kven-djöfull Djævel af en Kvinde.
-ræfill=kven-snift.
-skass arrig Kvinde, Arrigtrold, Heks, Rivejærn—shrew, vixen.
-*skinn Fruentimmer, Kvindemenneske.
-*skratti ond Kvinde—wicked woman, termagant.
-snift=*kvensa*—worthless woman.
-val udmærket, fortræffelig Kvinde—excellent woman.
-vargur=*kven-skass*
-væfla svag Kvinde.
mann-aumingi sölle Menneske, Stakkel—poor wretch.
-djöfull Djævel i Menneskeskikkelse—fiend of a man, scoundrel.
-fáráður Stakkel.
-*fýla Slubbert, Skurk, Umenneske—dirty fellow, scoundrel, rascal.
-*fjandi=*mann-fýla*—human fiend.
-furða en Mand, som er mere end almindelige Mennesker.
-gauð Kujon, Kryster.
-*gersemi fortræffeligt Menneske.
-hrak Skurk, Udskud af Menneskeheden—scoundrel, wretch.
-hræða human (or living) soul.
-*hundur Kæltring, Skurk, Afskum—dog of a man, rascal.
-kerti 1) fortrinligt Menneske, 2) Praas af et Menneske, sölle Fyr.
-kind=*mann-rola*.
-leysa 1) dáðlaus maður, ómenni, 2) afllaus maður—good-for-nothing fellow.
-*leysi = *mann-leysa*.
-lera Kryster, Drog—coward.
-*lydda = mann-lera.
-lirfa Dögenigt, Drog.
-*læra = *mann-lydda*.
-*níðingur = mann-hundur—miscreant, dastard.
-rýja sölle Skrog.
-ræfill sölle Djævel.
-skauð Dögenigt—good-for-nothing fellow.
-*skelmir Skarnsmenneske—rascal, rogue.
-*skepna = *mann-rola*—poor fellow.
-*skratti Slyngel—rascal.
-*skræfa = *mann-skauð*—miserable coward.
-skömm = *mann-fýla*—rascal.
-svín Svinebæst.
-*tetur, -tötur, stakkels Menneske—poor wretch.

COMPOUNDS OF THE *Mann-skratti* TYPE

-tuska = mann-tötur.
-val udsögte Folk, Elite.

From memory I can supply the following words in addition to the above:

mann-andskotinn the devil of a man, the son of a bitch.
-árinn same, but much weaker.
-asninn the ass of a man, the fool.
-bjálfinn the fool of a man, the fool.
-garmurinn the poor (dog of a) man.
-greyið the poor (dog of a) fellow.
-hróið the poor fellow.
-hræið the poor (dog, originally 'corpse' of a) fellow.
-ómyndin the good-for-nothing fellow.
-ótuktin the scoundrel, the no-good so and so.
-skollinn = mann-árinn.
-skrambinn = mann-árinn.
-ves(a)lingurinn the wretch of a man, the poor fellow.

In the preceding I have for practical reasons restricted the investigation to compounds with 'woman' (*kvenn-*) and 'man' (*mann-*), or 'girl' and 'boy,' as a first part of the compound. I have done this because of the fact that, since these compounds are used in terms of endearment, pity, and scolding, they would most likely be found with a first element referring to a person.

Still, these compounds are far from being restricted to persons alone; they can also be used concerning animals and any familiar object. Since searching for instances of this kind in the dictionaries like Cleasby-Vigfússon, Fritzner, and Blöndal would be a laborious task, I have chosen to give excerpts from two writers of colloquial prose who for stylistic reasons employ these compounds to a considerable extent.

The first author is Jón Thoroddsen (1818-68), whose language has been investigated by Steingrímur J. Þorsteinsson in *Jón Thoroddsen og skáldsögur hans*, II, 586-91. There are ninety-five instances in Thoroddsen's three works: *Dálítil ferðasaga*,

COMPOUNDS OF THE *Mann-skratti* TYPE

Piltur og stúlka, and *Maður og kona*. I classify them according to the first element.

PERSONS: *pilt-kind, kerlingar-vargur, barna-grey, kerlingar-hrotur, bónda-kind, krakka-orma-anga-nóran, krakka-orma-anga-nóruskinns-greyið, konu-mynd, kvennmanns-ræfill, kerlingar-skepna, króa-skinnin, mann-skömm, ráðskonu-ský, vinnumanns-tetur, mann-tötrið, kerlingar-andstyggð, strák-óhræsið, mann-fýla, kerlingar-grey, karl-hólkur, barna-hró, karla-hró, karlmannshræða, mann-kind, stúlku-kind, foreldra-myndir, meðhjálparamynd, systur-mynd, mann-ræfill, mann-skepna, krakka-skinn, karl-skrunka, kvenn-snift, dreng-tetur, stúlku-tetur, Tuddatetur, kvenn-væfla.*

Tudda-tetur shows a personal name (nickname) as a first element.

ANIMALS: *hest-skrattinn, lamb-kettlingur, hunda-vargar.*
PET NAMES: *grey-skammirnar, garm-skinn.*
PARTS OF THE HUMAN BODY: *lúku-grey, mjaðmar-grey, sálargrey, lappar-skarnið, lúku-skarn, sálar-skarn, skrokk-skrifli, skallaskömm.*
CLOTHING: *klút-bleðill, blöðku-visk, klút-skræpur, skinnkoddableðill, peysu-garmur, húfu-pottlok.*
FOOD: *mjaðar-skömm, köku-blaðkur, köku-bleðill, kjötsúpu-gutl, súpu-sopi, bita-tætla.*
SICKNESS: *heima-konu-fjandi, heimakonu-skratti.*
INSTRUMENTS: *tunnu-grey, kút-hola, kistil-korn, keralds-kríli, hellublaðkur, kúpu-hola, kvarnar-kind, poka-snigill.*
LETTERS: *bréf-grey, bréf-skömm, sendibréfs-korn, bréf-mið, blaðsneypa.*
HOUSES AND PARTS: *skemmugrey, kofa-hró, baðstofukofa-mynd, skemmu-skrifli, hús-kytra, geilar-skömm.*
ESTATES: *jarðar-skinn, jarðar-tetur, jarðar-þúfa.*
FEATURES IN LANDSCAPE: *heiðar-greyið, læk-sytra, tún-skiki.*
TOWNS: *Víkur-greyið, Víkur-skömm*, i.e. *Reykjavík.*
VERBAL-ABSTRACT: *bú-hokur.*

The collection from the first sixty-eight pages of Guðmundur G. Hagalín, *Kristrún í Hamravík*, is as follows:

PERSONS: *húsmóður-nefnan* (=ég), *stúlku-tetur, stúlku-kindin, móður-myndin, Anítu-skinn, barn-ungarnir, sýslumanns-kindin, hreppstjóra-tetrið Anítu-tetur, húsmóður-ómyndin, kvennstelpa, nánasar-ódýr, telpu-kindin, kerlingar-hrota, Anítu-hró, kvenn-kindur, húsmóður-mynd.*

[55]

COMPOUNDS OF THE *Mann-skratti* TYPE

ANIMALS: *Kattar-kvikindið, læðu-greyið, fugls-aumingi, ígulkersódó* (=*ótó*), *læðu-smánin, kálf-greyið, kálf-smánin.*
CLOTHES: *pils-gopi, buxna-myndirnar, spari-garmar* (=*sparifatagarmar*), *sængur-tila.*
FOOD: *ket-tæja.*
SICKNESS: *heilsu-slitur, innflúenzu-skolli, billa-skollin, landfarasóttar-ótukt, uppgerðar-vella, þela-skömm, gigtar-forsmánin.*
INSTRUMENTS: *nálar-grey, rúm-korn, prjóna-greyin, kútholu-greyið, stól-skömm, prjóna-skammirnar, krúsar-kvölin, krúsar-greyið, krúsar-tetrið, krúsar-skömmin, prjóna-smánir, gleraugnagarmar.*
HOUSE AND PARTS: *baðstofu-hró, stoðar-grey, verbúðar-ræfill.*
LAND: *veraldar-hali.*
VERBAL-ABSTRACT: *bú-hokur.*
DIMINUTIVA: *agnar-vitund, agnar-kvölin, hugmyndar-óvera.*

It would be of real interest to classify these words according to the amount and kind of emotion which they express. We would find that they express praise, open (*kvenn-skörungur*) and concealed (*húsmóður-myndin*=*ég*), pity (*mann-auminginn*), condescension (*stúlku-kind*), disdain (*mann-skræfan*), spite (*kerlingar-vargurinn*), and black hate (*mann-andskotinn*), the last compound representing Icelandic cursing. Still, the task would be far from easy, for the emotional value of the words varies greatly from person to person. Such an analysis cannot be attempted here, but must await future investigation.

REFERENCES

1. Since this was written, I have found the following in German: "Nicht weniger gut unterrichtet ist er über den Schaden, den der Körper des Wärwolfs in der Stadt anrichtet, als Pantagruel ihn über die Mauer geworfen hat. Er weiss genau, dass er auf dem Marktplatz wie ein Frosch platt auf den Bauch fiel, und im Falle just einen verbrannten Kater, eine nasse Katze, ein *Nonnenfürzchen* und ein aufgezäumtes Gänschen tot schlug."— Heinrich Schneegans, *Geschichte der grotesken Satire* (Strassburg, 1894), p. 191.

The Runes of Kensington

ERIK WAHLGREN

University of California, Los Angeles

THE PRESENT PAPER has been called forth by recent discussion of the Kensington stone and in particular by S. N. Hagen's long and carefully documented article in *Speculum*.[1] No attempt at a similar apparatus will be made here. A vast amount has been published on the Kensington stone; a collection of these sources would unduly burden the present article. The standard treatises on runes, together with Noreen's *Altschwedische Grammatik*, will suffice for most purposes.[2] A disadvantage of the present publication is the printing difficulty of reproducing runes, particularly the innovations found in the Kensington alphabet.[3] For this reason, the article is abridged by as much space as might have been devoted to epigraphical details. Any lack of perspicuity resulting from the deletion of the runic symbols themselves may be minimized by reference to Hagen's clearly drawn runic alphabets.[4] In company with him, I shall pay no attention to the circumstances of the find, the physical character of the carving, or to geographical and dendrological details, since there is substantial agreement that the *language* of the inscription must be the final determinant.

As transliterated by Professor Hagen, the inscription (with line-numbers added) reads as follows:

1. 8: göter: ok: 22: norrmen: po:
2. [þen]o: opþagelsefarþ: fro:
3. winlanþ: of: west: wi:
4. haþe: läger: weþ: 2: skjar: en:
5. þags: rise: norr fro: þeno: sten:
6. wi: war: ok: fiske: en: þagh: äptir:
7. wi: kom: hem: fan: 10: man: röþe:
8. af: bloþ: og: þeþ: AVM:

[57]

9. fräelse: af: illy:
10. här: 10: mans: we: hawet: at: se:
11. äptir: wore: skip: 14: þagh: rise:
12. from: þeno: öh: ahr: 1362:

For this text, departing in several particulars from the renderings of Holand and others, Hagen supplies the following translation:

1. Eight Götlanders and twenty-two Norwegians on
2. [this] exploration-journey from
3. Vinland over the west. We
4. had camp beside two sheds, one
5. day's journey north from this stone.
6. We were and fished one day; after
7. we came home, found ten men red
8. with blood and tortured. Hail, Mary!
9. Deliver from evil!
10. Have ten men by the sea to look
11. after our ships, fourteen-day journey
12. from this island. Year, 1362.

Hagen complains of the "chain reaction" set up by the famous telegram sent from Christiania in 1899 by three Norwegian scholars, in which the Kensington stone was pronounced a modern forgery, chiefly as he states, because it was supposed to contain certain English words. He reasons that if the "Anglicisms" can be explained away, a half-century of unwarranted prejudice against the inscription will be overcome. The problem of whether the words *of* and *from* and *þeþ* are essentially English has, however, next to no importance for an identification of the language of the inscription. In my opinion, that language is unmistakably modern Scandinavian, presumably a nineteenth century Swedish dialect, contaminated by other elements (Norwegian? English?), and indiscriminately "touched-up" with archaicizing features, the whole adapted to a partly borrowed, partly home-made runic series, and carved by a person or persons unknown, this only a few years before the stone's discovery in

1898. Seen in this light, the inscription makes philological sense. From the point of view of fourteenth century Scandinavian, it does not. I am merely re-stating what numerous foreign and domestic scholars have previously asserted. All too apparently, the thesis has needed this re-stating.[5]

In the following pages I shall make some general observations on the inscription and then proceed to a discussion of Hagen's principal arguments.

Considered as a linguistic document purporting to be six hundred years old, the Kensington inscription is unique for its alphabet, for its vocabulary, and for its grammar. Almost every one of its features is exceptional, if the recorded literature of the fourteenth century be allowed to give testimony in the philological courts. Of the twenty-three runic characters which we can identify, but which cannot be reproduced here (I refer again to Hagen's excellent drawings[6]), fewer than half could be called normal or "regular" runes, namely the symbols (considered in the Latin order) for *b, h, i, l, m, p, r, s, t* (with qualifications), *þ*. The symbol for *g* is normal only if we label it a "reverse rune." The runes for *e* and *o* approach the normal, at least. Those for *a* and *k* are unique, the signs for *v* and *y* are quite anomalous, and the characters representing *æ (ä), ø (ö), n,* and *j* are utterly impossible. Let me explain further. The symbol for *a* (resembling a Latin X) would be a pronounced innovation even without the hook so clearly projecting from the right arm. This hook serves no conceivable function of distinguishment;[7] it has no known antecedents and is quite out of keeping with all evidence as to runic development and tradition; it does make capital sense as the whim of a subliterate nineteenth century antiquarian. The symbol for *k* comes under strong suspicion at once in view of its being a reverse *k* from our Latin alphabet. But the evidence condemns it still further, for whereas in any "reputable" runic series

[59]

the symbols for *g* and *k* stand in intimate relationship, *g* being characteristically distinguished from *k* by the addition of a dot, the relationship between these two symbols on the Kensington stone reveals comfortable ignorance of any such expectations. The symbols have been arbitrarily created, without due regard for that logic and economy of effort which bespeak somewhat more than a chance connection with a given runic tradition. As for runic *v* (Hagen's *w*), in a normal sequence of runes it would appear as a slight modification, by means of a dot, of its near relative, the symbol for *f*. Adopting the technique of the dot, and grievously misapplying it, the inscription makes *v* into a near twin of *m*! This feature alone, so utterly alien to runic conceptions throughout centuries of development, would suffice to bring an otherwise acceptable inscription into disrepute. But there is worse to come. I refer to the clearly *umlauted* characters for *y*, *æ*, and *ø* (in addition to which umlauts the crossbar on *y* and the slanted cross inside the circle of the *ø* simply out-Herod Herod). Now the use of two dots above a vowel to signify mutation is too recent a practice to be reflected in a genuine document from 1362. The *ö* and *ä* symbols with two dots were not in use in Scandinavia before the sixteenth century, not even in manuscripts, let alone carvings in rock.[8] Their appearance on the Kensington stone is fatal for its authenticity. We come then to the *j*-rune, a pure impossibility in *any* kind of document from the fourteenth century, since it is known to have been invented by the Frenchman P. Ramus in the sixteenth century.[9] No genuine rune stone contains a separate symbol for *j*, consonantal *i* not being distinguished in the inscriptions from vocalic *i*. To be sure, this symbol is quite in its element among the ingenuities of the Kensington monument. But though we have leveled a charge of excessive modernity at this inscription, yet we may console the Smithsonian Institution (present home of the controversial stone) by pointing out that this unique inscription from 1362 does possess one redeeming archaic feature: an *n*-rune with crossbar passing completely through the upright stave and forming thus a runic character of the type which, on Erik Moltke's very good authority, was never used after the year 1100.[10]

Though the preceding objections reflect a set of facts sufficient of themselves to brand the Kensington stone as a forgery from beginning to end, they by no means exhaust the supply of objections to it. Let us look briefly at the vocabulary and the spelling. The word *norrmen* is found in suspiciously modern dress, whereas in such an inscription the spelling *norþmen* (*norðmen*) or *normen* would have been expected.[11] The word *oppagelsefarþ*, the curious spelling of whose last element more clearly points to a mistaken linguistic surmise on the part of a nineteenth century dabbler than to orthographic practices (or pronunciation) five hundred years earlier, has won attention from all critics. Every argument that I have seen hitherto put forth in defense of this word as a fourteenth century product is based on a misrepresentation or at least a misunderstanding of the facts. It is fatal for the genuineness of our inscription that the Swedish word *uppdaga* preserved until the end of the eighteenth century a meaning entirely different from that required here. The verb meant *bli dager, bli ljust* ('to dawn,' 'grow light'). According to Jansson, Atterbom was the first to use the verb in the sense of *upptäcka* ('discover').[12] Furthermore, the very term "voyage of exploration," though taken for granted by modern men, is too utterly self-conscious an expression to have been used by a medieval Scandinavian, especially if he himself were the "explorer." Hagen's citation of Storm on this issue has no pertinence whatever.[13] Certainly the men of the Viking Age and their descendants sought out and explored new lands, as the discoveries of Iceland, Greenland, and Vinland bear ample witness.

They were explorers in the true sense. But there is no evidence to show that they ever referred to themselves as such. Professor Flom's statement of forty years ago is fully valid.[14] If we look again at the word *opþagelsefarþ* we find the very late element *opdagelse* (a good Dano-Norwegian word!) combined with an unmutated form *farþ* (from *farði), which must be incredibly old—a ridiculous combination. The word is a patent latter-day forgery, and barring a confession from the grave, we could not ask for more evidence.

The word or words appearing as (*en*) *þags rise* and as (*14*) *þagh rise* constitute another stumbling block to a fourteenth century origin for the Kensington inscription. The combined testimony of Söderwall's dictionary of Middle Swedish and of the Swedish Academy's dictionary of the language based on historical principles is that the word *dagsresa* was not in use before 1599.[15] If we continue to have "some slight respect for paleographical evidence,"[16] we shall not feel constrained to see in this fact some sort of proof that the word had lived underground for the 250 years (actually, a much longer period would have to be supposed) required to authenticate this inscription. The evidence of the Kensington stone is here no evidence at all until the stone itself is reasonably authenticated. Söderwall lists *daghs ledh* (modern Swedish *dagsled* 'a day's travel') in a meaning appropriate to the Kensington inscription.[17] The author of the inscription simply made a poor choice of words. Once again we are confronted with a modernism.

The presumed Anglicisms *of, fro, from þeþ, illy* (not *rise*!) may, any or all of them, be such, or they may simply evidence in yet another way the Minnesota pioneer's desire to create the illusion of older forms and his inability to do so for want of learning and works of reference. *Of* and *fro* look like deliberate attempted reconstructions; *illy* and *þeþ* are doubtful; *from* is not out of place in the language of Minnesota.[18] It is unlikely that this particular question can be solved, and it is in fact unimportant to our thesis except to emphasize once more the multitude of inconsistencies barring the inscription's claim to medieval origin. It is unnecessary to account for these borrowings or bastard forms, for nowhere are they more appropriate than among the homemade runic symbols from a Minnesota farm. I may point out an additional idiosyncrasy in the Kensington inscription: as I read it, it employs not a single *abbreviation*, not even the *m*-rune for the equivalent of "man, men," unless the word *fro* (twice in this spelling) is an abbreviation for *from* (appearing once). This affords additional help in appraising the language of the inscription.

The subject of the grammar of the Kensington inscription has been covered many times. The *uniform* use of singular verbs instead of plurals, in a purported medieval text, cannot pass unchallenged when even today the problem of whether to use singular or plural verb forms perplexes all writers of Swedish. It is well established that cultural isolates tend to adhere to conservative linguistic forms. A medieval Northman capable of carving a runic message at all would have known the written language, the spelling, the vocabulary appropriate to it. He would most certainly have clung to the tried and true, i.e., the conservative manner of runecarving that he had learned at home.[19] A form like *havet* (or *hawet*) for the correct neut. sing. dat. form *hafinu* drives home the point we have been reiterating: in regard to neither the runic alphabet nor the grammar and orthography of Old Swedish was the Minnesota dabbler in runic lore sophisticated enough to convey through his carvings even the slightest impression of antiquity.

We turn now to the article by Hagen, whose main contentions have been refuted, I make bold to assert, by the analysis above. I select here a few points for additional rebuttal. By way of novelty, Hagen identifies the word *skjar* of the rune stone not with dat. plur. *skæriom*, modern Swedish *skär* 'rocky islets,' 'skerries,' as usually proposed in this connection, but with ON., OIcel. *skjá*, fem. gender, purportedly meaning 'shed' and the ancestor of modern Norwegian dialect *skjaa*, masc. gender, referring to a type of shed, usually without walls, used for drying.[20] The word is unknown to me in Swedish although ultimately related to *skjul* 'shed, shelter.' Assuming that N. *skjaa* 'shed' (there is also a N. *skjaa* referring to a membrane, especially one stretched taut to serve as a window pane) is in any way concerned here, and that *skjar* is intended as its plural, Hagen has furnished us with one more indication of the inscription's modernity, plus additional evidence for the hypothesis of Norwegian contamination. But as a fourteenth century word it is suspect. An OSw. *skjá cannot be established; the only *skjá* (*r*) I can locate in the standard dictionaries of ON., OIcel. is the ancestor of the N. word meaning 'membrane, window etc.'; and in any Scandinavian dialect from 1362 the word should show some trace of the dative plural ending -*m* so decisively lacking here, but definitely required in a locative use with the preposition *veþ* (OSw. *viþ, vit*) of the inscription. Hagen's assumption of an accusative plural ending here is incorrect. A similar grammatical blunder in the inscription appears in the modern (N. or Sw.) combination *wore skip* in the phrase *at se äptir wore skip*. This is assuming that the phrase could have been used at all in that sense during the fourteenth century.

Likewise suspect is Hagen's attempt to translate *þeþ* as 'tortured' and to give it grammatical warrant. His argument begs the question, and it affords misinformation to boot. In the meaning of English 'dead,' *þeþ* has the advantage of making sense at once, without elaborate argument; the odds are certainly in favor of such an explanation.

What does Hagen mean by the sentence: "Once more I want to point to the fact that the inscriber never fails to use his ö-sign in all the three words which we know had ö in the fourteenth century"?[21] If he is referring to the phonetic value represented by the phonetic symbol ø, he should say so. If he means literally that o-umlaut (ö) was used in the fourteenth century, he is sadly mistaken.

In his discussion of the word ferþ:farþir [færþ], Hagen misapplies and partially suppresses Professor Noreen's statement in *Aschwed. Gram.*; cf. par. 63.1: "Nur umgelautete formen in *færþ* (*farði-*), gen. *færþar* statt *farþar* fahrt"; cf. par. 406, paradigm. Hagen's argument is fallacious in that he confuses the singular with the plural.[22] An (occasional) nom. plur. form *farþir*, without umlaut, is slender evidence for a nom. (or dat.) sing. form without umlaut; at least Noreen has not implied any such thing. What evidence is there for Hagen's statement that "the inscriber did not forget his dots for the very good reason that he wrote the word (*-farþ*) as he pronounced it"? If, during the fourteenth century or subsequently, the word was ever pronounced as here suggested, it has left no trace behind in the spelling and pronunciation of today (*färd*), which are evidence of a consistent trend since early times.[23]

The discussion of *10 mans* is largely meaningless, and the sentence "*10 manns* is still current in Modern Icelandic" confuses the issue by implying that the collective form *10 manns* is a survival of the form once preferred over *10 manna* or *10 menn*.[24] That would be hard to show, in my opinion. Adverting once more to *þeþ*, Hagen tries to explain it as a dittographic error. Such an error is possible in paper or vellum manuscripts but unlikely for the laborious chiseling of letters in stone, except on one hypothesis: the (modern) runemaster worked mechanically on the basis of a text prepared beforehand— and poorly prepared— on paper.

The citing of Storm's views on fourteenth century voyaging impels one to inquire how much positive proof we have that Paul Knutsson's "command voyage" ever took place.[25] Are the historians satisfied on this point? And if it did take place, did the voyagers ever get beyond Greenland? Hagen now proceeds to quote Noreen on the development of OSw. *hadhe* out of *hafðe* as evidence of fourteenth century writing of the singular of this verb in place of the plural.[26] But Noreen (*Aschwed. Gram.*, par. 306.2) here translates this form as a singular (*hatte*, not *hatten*)! Another dubious statement is the following: "The early use of singular forms for plurals is *not confined* [italics mine] to Swedish and Norwegian. In Old Danish the situation is much the same." The relative *conservatism* of Swedish is well known. Hagen correctly reads, in the Kensington inscription, *här* for *har*. I am reluctant to take this seriously as a "variant form," quite apart from the incongruity of an umlaut in a medieval text. As an absent-minded mistake it is, moreover, not uncommon in modern Swedish.

In the phrase *wi war ok fiske* of the Kensington inscription, *ok* is an example of a type of overcompensation. Hagen claims it for antiquity but can adduce no satisfactory date of provenience. He regards it as explained, in this specific instance, by the carelessness of "rapid speech." Runes are not carved at the rate of "rapid speech." It comports with everything else we know about the inscription to regard the phrase as modern Swedish *talspråk*.

Professor Hagen refers often to "the inscriber's dialect." This dialect is an amorphous thing, without shape or beginning or end. He wastes considerable space in discussing the impossible demonstrative form *þeno,* conceivably a (rare) neut. sing. dat.

form here used with both a *feminine* and a *masculine* noun (*fro þeno sten*, mistakenly for *fra þessum steni*; and *from þeno öh* for *fra þessi ø*; and if Hagen's restored text is correct, *þeno* modifies another feminine word in the phrase *po* [*þen*]*o opþagelse-farþ*!). And immediately he adds: "It would be interesting to know whether the inscriber would also have said *fro þeno hus* 'from this house'" (p. 338)! And perhaps, in the "inscriber's dialect," *þætta pigha* would also have been correct? One never can tell about a dialect as wild as this one. Hagen explains *þeno*, naturally, as a blend, Q.E.D. When all else fails, this must be the explanation. Now, blends and contaminations of various kinds are commonplaces in linguistic history, and as a rule they can be traced. But in a document whose every line breathes forgery, this mode of reasoning is worthless. Hagen sarcastically inquires where "our forger" found the form *þeno*—surely not in "Noreen's *Altschwedische Grammatik*, for this was not yet published."[27] Scholarship in the field of Old Swedish long antedated Noreen. But nobody has accused "our forger" of undue familiarity with that scholarship.

On p. 341 Hagen states: "I suspect that not all fourteenth-century Swedes were familiar with fourteenth-century runic writing." He is here attempting to explain certain archaic features in the Kensington inscription. This is indeed an argument for a presumed conservatism, rather than modernism, in the inscription. And it comports ill indeed with Hagen's insistence throughout on the relative modernity, for the fourteenth century, of the inscription, with syncope of inconvenient vowels, singular verb forms that reflect oral discourse rather than conservative literary tradition, etc. But while the carver of runes was, in Hagen's supposition, runically untutored and not abreast of his age, he seems on the other hand to have been phonetically acute to an extraordinary degree, likewise according to Hagen, who gives full details. As a phonetician this early Swede was fantastically ahead of his time. Nor does Hagen find any essential lack of harmony between the adoption of "a number of Latin letters, some of them more or less modified in order to make them fit, *after a fashion*, into runic surroundings," and the archaic approach just referred to.[28] The truth is that common sense, consistency, a recognition of the fact that runic writings follow observable patterns and belong to a definable tradition—such criteria are to Hagen inadmissible. "We cannot assume," he writes, "that all runic writings have come down to us." Indeed, as all runologists know, many runic monuments have perished. "In the fourteenth century there must *still have existed* [italics mine] a considerable number of perpetual calendars with runic signs." But the earliest one known in Sweden is from 1328, and it was reproduced in print in the seventeenth century; a familiarity with these runic calendars continued in some places until the end of the last century. "The inscriber's use of the pentadic numerals shows that he was not ignorant of calendars." This reflects a chain of thought that might have been pursued with profit. For the similarity of the Kensington runes to those found on late Swedish farm calendars has been remarked again and again. But Hagen spends much time in finding "runic" antecedents for the numerals of the Kensington stone. These numerical symbols are simple and natural, quite in keeping with what one would expect in an ignorant man's late forgery, and totally unworthy of serious discussion.

No one of those who have presumed to employ "scholarly" evidence in support of the genuineness of the Kensington stone has avoided the pitfalls that lurk in every line of its inscription. Unproved assertions, naïve hopes, twisted citations, misread authorities are the "scholarly" tools employed; an isolated, piecemeal examination of each individual word and "rune," without reference to corporate incongruities, comprises the "methodology"; a bitter determination to prove a thesis in defiance of stubborn facts constitutes the apparent goal.[29]

REFERENCES

1. S. N. Hagen, "The Kensington Runic Inscription," *Speculum*, XXV (1950), 321-56.
2. Noreen, *Altschwedische Grammatik*, Halle (1904).
3. The latter may indeed safely be thought of as an alphabet rather than a *futhark*.
4. Hagen, *op. cit.*, p. 342. This discussion has been materially aided by Hagen's transliteration of the inscription, p. 322, his translation, p. 323, and the two photographic reproductions, opposite pp. 321 and 333, respectively.
5. The writer records here his debt to Docent Sven B. F. Jansson of Stockholm University for a personal exchange of views on the Kensington stone early in 1949 and for the latter's telling article, " 'Runstenen' från Kensington i Minnesota," *Nordisk tidskrift för vetenskap, konst och industri*, XXV (1949), 377-405.
6. Hagen, p. 342.
7. Hagen's rationalization of this feature is fanciful.
8. I refer to Jansson's article in which, although devoting but little space to the aspect of the runes themselves, he quotes (pp. 388-89) from a newspaper article by the Danish runologist Erik Moltke on exactly this point.
9. See the preceding note. As these Scandinavian specialists have demonstrated beyond cavil, the arguments of Holand and his followers are based—here as elsewhere—on faulty manuscript readings.
10. " 'Vi har med andre ord for os en runemester, der på den ene side anvender en rune (*n*), der var uddød o. 1100, på den anden side bruger tegn *-j* og *ö-*, der først kom til verden o. 1550, og stenen daterer sig selv til 1362!' " Quoted in Jansson's article, p. 389.
11. Cf. Noreen, *op. cit.*, par. 308.1.
12. Jansson, p. 395. P. D. A. Atterbom, poet and professor, lived 1790-1855.
13. Hagen, pp. 331-32.
14. "The conception 'journey of exploration' did not and could not exist in 1362" (G. T. Flom, "The Kensington Rune Stone. A Modern Inscription from Douglas County, Minnesota, *Transactions of the Illinois State Historical Society for the Year 1910* [Springfield, Illinois, 1912], p. 117). This is quoted from Hagen, p. 330 and footnote 39, since the volume in question is not available to me.
15. K. F. Söderwall, *Ordbok öfver svenska medeltidsspråket* (Lund, 1884-86), *s. v.*; *Ordbok över svenska språket utgiven av Svenska Akademien* (Lund, 1898-), *s. v.*
16. The quotation is from Hagen, p. 328.
17. Söderwall, *op. cit., s. v.* The word *resa* 'to raise' had originally only transitive meaning in OSw. The intransitive verb *resa* 'to travel' and the noun *resa* 'journey' are of later origin, apparently under MLG influence. Note that the OIcel. verb *reisa* is transitive: *reisa ferð* 'to start on a journey.' This information is derived from E. Hellquist, *Svensk etymologisk ordbok* (Lund, 1922), pp. 638-39, and Cleasby-Vigfusson, *An Icelandic-English Dictionary* (Oxford, 1874), p. 491. None of this is any evidence for the existence of the specific compound *dagsresa* (in any spelling) as early as 1362. Cf. OIcel. *dag-róðr, dag-sigling*, as listed by Cleasby-Vigfusson, p. 95.
18. I have been struck by the curious blend of English and Swedish to be found in Öhman's letter of 1909 to W. Upham, as reproduced by Jansson, p. 398. This is not to be taken for a surmise as to the rune-carver's identity.

[69]

19. Jansson, p. 402: "Det är inte lätt att återge talspråk i skrift. . . . Kunde han sin tids runskrift, så kunde han också sin tids skriftspråk—stavning, orförråd o. s. v. Han var väl ingen dialektupptecknare född 500 år för tidigt?"
20. Hagen, p. 325. I find *skjaa* listed in A. Torp, *Nynorsk etymologisk ordbok* (Kristiania, 1919), as reported by Hagen, and likewise in Hj. Falk and A. Torp, *Etymologisk ordbok over det norske og det danske sprog. Andet Bind. N-Ø* (Kristiania, 1906), s. v. "Skur I . . . dertil n. dial. *skjaa,* m., oldn. *skjá,* f. skur'. "But reference to the standard Old Norse and Old Icelandic dictionaries by L. Heggstad, Fritzner, Þorkelsson, F. Jónsson, and Cleasby-Vigfusson, coupled with F. Holthausen, *Vergleichendes und etymologisches Wörterbuch des Altwestnordischen* (Göttingen, 1948), shows no feminine word *skjá* meaning 'shed' and the like, but only the masculine word *skjár* (plur. *skjár, skjáir,* according to Heggstad), in the sense of a stretched membrane used as a window (in the roof) of dwellings. This meaning is preserved in the masculine word *skjaa* listed in Torp and Falk-Torp, above, and is the only word found in M. Skard, *Nynorsk ordbok for rettskrivning og litteraturlesnad* (Kristiania, 1912). I have not looked further for *skjá* 'shed.' In this connection a non-philological, but definitely practical, objection occurs to me against the translation 'sheds' for *skjar,* in the Kensington inscription. It seems most doubtful that a party of skilled explorers, wary and alone in potentially hostile territory, would have made camp so near to human habitations.
21. Hagen, p. 326.
22. Hagen, p. 328.
23. *Ibid.* The possibility of leveling out in the *i*-stems has not been overlooked. But this is a negative argument at best.
24. Hagen, p. 329.
25. Hagen, pp. 331-32.
26. Hagen, p. 333.
27. Hagen, p. 338.
28. Hagen, p. 341. The italics are mine.
29. Even the alleged "hardness" of the graywacke (Hagen, p. 339) fails to conform to the description of graywacke found in Merriam's unabridged *Webster* (Springfield, Mass., 1942) or in Sir A. Geikie, *Geology* (N. Y., 1904), pp. 157-58, nor to Jansson's description of it as "en jämförelsevis mjuk stenart" (Jansson, p. 379), after a personal inspection of the Kensington stone.

Two Unrecognized Celtic Names:
Vagn Akason and Thorvald Tintein

Lee M. Hollander

University of Texas

In Vagn Ákason the stirring *Jómsvíkinga Saga* has set before us one of the most dashing heroes of literature—the very embodiment of the Viking Age. But though unforgettable, Vagn is far from being one of the main characters in that saga all compact of the intrigues of kings and the derring-do of bold buccaneers involving the destinies of whole countries and culminating in the terrific sea-battle of Hjǫrungavág. Significantly, however, it is this very Vagn who by his name is largely responsible for the defeat of the Jómsvíkings' attempt to conquer Norway.

At a big banquet to which the Jómsvíkings have been lured by King Svein Forkbeard of Denmark their leader, Sigvaldi, when half-drunk vows to conquer Norway and drive out its ruler, Earl Hákon. Heeding the sage advice of Sigvaldi's spouse, the Jómsvíking fleet, reinforced by sixty vessels of the king, immediately leaves the feast to fall upon Earl Hákon unawares. But when the Jómsvíkings overrun and sack Tunsberg—in the hope, perhaps, of capturing Hákon there—a certain yeoman, Geirmund (or Ogmund) by name, thwarts their purpose: After valiantly defending himself in a loft, he leaps down into the street. Vagn happens to be standing close by and slashes off his hand above the wrist. Relinquishing it to Vagn, Geirmund manages to escape to the woods. From there, he overhears what is said to Vagn when he picks up the large ring which went with the hand: *fénaði þér nú, Vagn* ("There you made a haul, Vagn"), thus betraying who the invaders are. Traveling day and night, Geirmund makes his way to Earl Hákon and forewarns him of their approach, in time for Hákon hastily to gather a fleet sufficient to cope with them.

Thus in substance the versions of the saga preserved in MSS. *AM* 291, 4to; *AM* 510, 4to; *Holm.* 7, 4to; and *Flateyarbók* I, 183f.

In the *Fagrskinna* version this episode is told somewhat differently—and less well. There, after losing his hand to Vagn, Geirmund makes for the sea, procures a boat, mans it, "and sailed till he found Earl Hákon. Geirmund had heard the names of the Jómsvíkings and of Vagn mentioned when he escaped and said that Vagn took but a small bite—*Vagn var smábeitr*—when he hewed off no more than the hand of the man who stood before him."

Discussing this episode, with special reference to the name of Vagn, Magnus Olsen in a recent paper[1] from the remark *Vagn var smábeitr* draws far-reaching and daring conclusions; viz., that the name of Vagn is the same as that of the grampus or killer-whale (*Orca gladiator*), the tiger of the northern seas; that this name fitted him exactly (he is described as utterly ruthless and unmanageable—*úeirinn*—and as having already at the age of nine killed three men); and that the *Fagrskinna* version, as compared to the others in which Vagn's greed rather than his bloodthirstiness is brought out, originated in western Norway, where the grampus was well known and the allusion to it in the phrase quoted was understood.

Now, contrary to Olsen[2] I would regard the remark *Vagn var smábeitr* as more naturally coming from a Jómsvíking jeering at Vagn, otherwise so redoubtable a fighter who killed with one fell blow, rather than from Geirmund himself standing before Earl Hákon and ruefully exhibiting his mutilated arm as confirmation of his tidings. Grant that, and Olsen's argument falls to the ground, because the grampus was probably unknown to most Danes,[3] whose field of operations lay chiefly in the Baltic, so that the allusion would not have been readily grasped by them. By the same token the inference of West Norwegian origin for the *Fagrskinna* version of the saga is deprived of its only, and slim, support.

Magnus Olsen cautiously does not with so many words say that Vagn bore his name because of his *vagn* nature; but he bolsters that assumption by adducing the fact that *ulfr* and *vargr* were appellations for both the animals and for criminals. However, many an honorable man was called Ulfr. And, besides, a person was said to be *ulfr, vargr* only after his deeds had revealed him as such. Real names were given at birth, when the nature of the man to be had not yet unfolded. How could such an ill-omened name as Vagn, if indeed it signified 'killer-whale,' be given the infant scion of the lord of Funen![4] The very fact that the name Vagn from the oldest times on was, and still is, borne by a considerable number of persons in Denmark[5]—and none in Norway, *nota bene*—forbids that assumption. Nor does that fact need to imply relation to our hero, even if we are told that *margt stórmenne er frá honum komit*—many persons of great account are descended from him.

But what then is the real meaning of the name Vagn? Formally it is identical with the Old Norse word for 'wain'; and indeed this meaning has been attributed to it and explained as due to the cultic significance of the chariot.[6] But that conjecture is hardly convincing![7]

It is far more plausible to assume that the name is of Celtic origin: Welsh *vachan, vahhan*, signifies 'little'; and this word used as a name in the forms Vaughan, Vaughn, Fawn, and the like is still borne by many families of Welsh origin.[8] The circumstance is to be kept in mind that according to the saga Vagn's family had connections in *Bretland* (Wales) His grandfather married a Welsh princess; and relations with Wales were maintained by him even after he had (again following the saga) founded the stronghold of Jómsborg on the Pomeranian coast. At his death he bequeathed his share of *Bretland* to Vagn, whom he loved dearly. It is true that there exist no historical data to support these statements of Welsh connections. Yet we know that Wales for centuries felt the fury of the Northmen and frequently allied itself with the intruders against the English.[9] So that it is by all means likely that the account of the saga reflects actual occurrences.

Quite apart from the origin of the name, however, Olsen may be right when he surmises that the remark *Vagn var smábeitr* contains a play on words. We must remember that the saga took ultimate shape in Iceland; and Icelanders have at all times been inveterate punsters, quick to note resemblances between form and content—such as here between Vagn's name and his ruthlessness resembling that of the grampus—and thus here to embody it in the incisive *Vagn var smábeitr*. Another example of punning comes to mind in the skald Kormák's derisively playing on the name of his successful rival for Steingerd, Thorvald Tintein. In stanza 32 of his *lausavísur* he speaks of the wretched *tindráttar maðr*—'that tin-puller,' and in stanza 39 he alludes to him *es tin tannar*, 'who chews tin,' and wonders why she ever was given to him.

It should, of course, have been suspected long ago that the name Tintein likewise is of Celtic origin. It has nothing to do with the metal tin. Cornish *Tinten* is derived either from *tin-tan*, 'the lower fortress,' or more likely, from *tin-den*, 'the stronghold on the hill.'[10] Anyone familiar with English place names will recall forms like Tintern, Tindale, Tintagel, Dinwiddy, etc., in which *tin* appears as the first element.[11] But it is unlikely that we shall ever know how Thorvald or one of his forebears[12] in the

TWO UNRECOGNIZED CELTIC NAMES

Skíðing family, prominent in Northern Iceland, came by his cognomen.

REFERENCES

1. *Maal og Minne*, 1943, pp. 181 f.
2. *Op. cit.*, p. 181, note 1.
3. Cf. Olsen's note, p. 187, on the range of the grampus.
4. But the giant Vagnhǫfði's name (*Jǫtna heiti* II, Finnur Jónsson, *Skjaldedigtning* I, þulur IVf) 'Grampus-head', Saxo's Vagnophtus, very likely, and appropriately, suggests his appearance.
5. See the new monumental collection *Danmarks gamle Personnavne* I, col. 1537-1541.
6. Thus already P. A. Munch, *Samlede Afhandlinger* 4, 196 f.; and, following him, H. Naumann, *Altnordische Namenstudien*, the work referred to in note 5, and R. Hornby, *Fornavne i Danmark i Middelalderen* (in *Personnavne, Nordisk Kultur*, VII), 1947, p. 193.
7. In Bechtel's *Die historischen Personennamen des Griechischen*, 1917, Klasse XI, I find nothing corresponding, though the chariot played a great role among the Greeks both in cultus and warfare.
8. See L'Estrange Ewen, *A History of the Surnames of the British Isles*, 1931; Bardsley, *A Dictionary of English and Welsh Surnames*, 1901. The name Bekan (also written Beigan), from the Old Irish form of the word, *becán* 'little,' occurs in *Landnámabók* 15, 23; 137, 34. Cf. Assar Janzén, *Personnavne* (*Nordisk Kultur*, VII), 1947, 139.
9. Cf. B. G. Charles, *Old Norse Relations with Wales*, 1934; esp. pp. 100-105.
10. Cf. R. S. Charnock, *Patronymica Cornu-Britannica*, 1870, p. 110; Eilert Ekwall, *The Concise Dictionary of English Place Names*, 1936, pp. 452-453.—Similar compounds appear in English place names like Highcastle, Oldcastle.
11. I surmise that the Icelandic name Tind, as, e.g., that of the skald Tindr Hallkelsson, also belongs here. (But of course not Norwegian place names like Tindset, Tinsjø, etc.)
12. Note that the name of his paternal uncle, Koðrán, likewise is of Celtic origin.

The Impact of English on American-Norwegian Letter Writing

EINAR HAUGEN

University of Wisconsin

1.1 In the course of his investigations of the American dialects of Norwegian (abbreviated AmN) the writer was fortunate enough to secure a goodly pack of letters addressed to the prominent Norwegian-language newspaper *Decorah-Posten* by its subscribers.[1] This newspaper, which appears weekly in Decorah, Iowa, has subscribers in every state of the Union, though the bulk of them are located in the Middle West. Its wide appeal is indicated by the fact that it has more subscribers than all other Norwegian-language newspapers in the country put together; in 1949 its paid circulation was 35,436. The sample of subscribers' letters here analyzed may seem small in comparison with the total number of subscribers, but their contents and style are highly representative of the writing skill of American speakers of Norwegian in the rural communities of the Middle West. These 289 letters written between January and July of 1936 run the gamut of the topics which occupy the contributors to the letter column in this paper, and they exemplify all the varied influences of the American environment on the immigrants. Their importance as linguistic evidence lies in the fact that they are entirely unretouched. This would not have been true of them after they appeared in the paper, where the editors regularly correct them into a form more consistent with their own orthographic and linguistic policies.

1.2 The states represented include the Midwestern homes of Norwegian immigrants: Minnesota 36.2%, Wisconsin 13.2%,

North Dakota 12.1%, South Dakota 7.3%, and Iowa 4.5%. There are also writers from the Far West, especially Washington (5.2%), and scattered individuals in many other states, all the way to Alaska. About four-fifths, or 78.5%, of the letters were written in a more or less successful approximation to the (Dano-) Norwegian language used by the paper. Another 16.3% (47 letters) were written in English; there were 11 letters in Danish, 2 in Swedish, and 2 in Norwegian dialect (or New Norse). Sixty-eight correspondents in all reported on their birthplace in Norway: of these 35.4% were from the Eastern Lowlands, 25% from the Eastern valleys (chiefly Gudbrandsdal), and 16.2% from the Trondheim region. This shows a predominance of East Norwegians over the Central and Western groups. Twenty-five mentioned their dates of immigration, which ranged from 1880 to 1924, the median being 1886. Eighteen gave their ages, which ranged from 67 to 92, the median being 76. Twelve stated how long they had subscribed to the paper, the median being 47 years. It is of course not valid to combine these figures, since they apply to different individuals; but they do give us a general picture of the kind of immigrants we are dealing with: men and women born in Eastern Norway in the 1860's and 1870's, who immigrated in the 80's and 90's and settled in the Middle West, where they have been reading *Decorah-Posten* ever since.

1.3 The purpose of this article will be to analyze the impact which English made on the Norwegian language of these immigrants, Americans of fifty years standing or more. The letters give abundant evidence of the gradual passing of the generation that was still capable of writing Norwegian. Many letters carry obituaries, those in English being usually accompanied by a request for translation into Norwegian. A few of the Norwegian letters show by their obvious anglicisms of construction and idiom that they were written by members of the younger generation whose Norwegian is rather shaky. Typical is the request of one writer that the editor correct her letter, as she 'har ikke gaaet paa norsk skole saa at sige untagen hvad Jeg har lært av min mor' (have not gone to Norwegian school so to speak except for what I learned from my mother). Even the handwriting shows American influence, for less than a hundred of the letters show any prominent trace of the more angular type of Norwegian school hand. Now and then Norwegian words are partly anglicized in spelling, e.g. femty (for *femti*) 'fifty,' uncel (for *onkel*) 'uncle'; and dates are often given in the American instead of the Norwegian form, e.g. June 1st for *1ste Juni*. Norwegian compounds are often written apart in the American fashion: reise penge, minde dag, kvinde forenings formand. Yet a total of 40% of the letters contained no anglicisms whatever, and another 23.6% showed no more than one per average page of 100 words. The absolute maximum for any writer was eight per page. This is modest enough in view of the circumstances. English may have modified the writers' mode of expression on many points, but they are still clearly writing Norwegian. Nothing approaching true linguistic confusion occurs, except in two brief and illiterate notes.

1.4 It is inevitable in a study like this that most of the examples of English influence will come from letters written by those who have the poorest command of writing in general. One who has been given a really thorough schooling in the spelling and the grammatical niceties of a language will usually try to avoid an adaptation which lays him open to the charge of not knowing the language. The less schooled writer will either be unaware of the standard of purity expected of him or be unable to live up to it. A few who are aware of it will deliberately violate it in the realization that the altered circumstances of an emigrated group require a modification of language patterns. Many who use anglicized forms in speech would hesitate to do so in writing. A rough index of the orthographic skill of the writers can be found in an investigation made of the spelling errors per page. Only one in twenty writers averaged less than one error per page (of a hundred words). About half of the writers committed from 1 to 5 errors per page, a third from 6 to 10, an eighth from 11 to 15. This estimate included errors in punctuation, capitalization, word spacing, and other such purely mechanical features. Many of the errors were of the same kind as have to be weeded out of the writing of Norwegian school children to this day—e.g., silent letters that are omitted, confusion of the letters *o* and *å*, *e* and *æ*, of the words *og* and *å*, or of single and geminated consonants.[2] Others were founded in the special difficulty of the country people in acquiring a spelling norm based on Danish rather than Norwegian traditions. Since most of our writers were of rural origin and emigrated from Norway at a time when the rural school system was not too effective, we are not surprised to find in their letters instances of dialect expression as well as non-standard forms and spellings.

1.5 The classification of loans here attempted will be based on the principles stated in the writer's article on 'The Analysis of Linguistic Borrowing' in *Language,* XXVI, 210-13 (1950). But the terminology there suggested has been partially modified in response to criticisms made by others and as a result of the writer's continued analysis of the material in preparing the manuscript of his book on *The Norwegian Language in America.* This writer holds that all borrowing results from an attempt by the speaker to reproduce in one language patterns previously heard in another language. In reproducing these patterns the speaker may import the foreign expression exactly as it was spoken, but he is more likely to substitute in some degree phonemes and morphemes from his own language which remind him of those he has heard. We may phrase this more precisely by saying that borrowing is a kind of linguistic REPRODUCTION which may be analyzed into IMPORTATION and SUBSTITUTION. A description of the process of borrowing (as distinct from the social backgrounds of borrowing) must be made in terms of the relation between these two procedures.

1.6 The usual terminology of borrowing distinguishes loanwords, semantic loans, loan translations or calques, and hybrid loans. For reasons explained in the above-mentioned article, the writer has attempted to set up a somewhat more consistent terminology. The term LOANWORD is retained, and the new terms LOANBLEND and LOANSHIFT have been coined to take the place of the somewhat inaccurate terms 'hybrid loan' and 'semantic loan.' A new analysis has also made it possible to include the loan translation under the latter term. A LOANWORD is defined as a loan which reproduces in part or whole the phonemic shape of the foreign model without coinciding with any previously existing expression in the language. A loanword which shows partial morphemic substitution may be called a LOANBLEND; an example is Pennsylvania German *blaumepai* 'plum pie,' in which *pai* is a loanword reproducing English *pie* by phonemic substitution, while *plum* has been reproduced by morphemic substitution of the German *blaum*. But whenever the morphemic substitution is complete and affects the entire word or expression, we have instead a LOANSHIFT, defined as any loan consisting of one or more native morphemes in a new context. If the shift is only one of social context, giving the native expression a new meaning, the loanshift is an EXTENSION, as in AmN *korn* which meant 'grain' in Norway, but 'Indian corn' in America. If the shift is also or primarily one of linguistic context, a new expression comes into being and we may call the loanshift a CREATION, as when English *butterfly* is reproduced by some American German speakers as *butterfliege*. Examples of these types found in our letters will be given in the following discussion, taken in the order in which they have been listed above.

1.7 The reader may miss any discussion of the meanings of the words borrowed, or analysis of the spheres of life in which they are primarily found. The present article is limited to the purely formal aspects of the borrowing process. To take up the social, non-linguistic aspects would require an entirely different approach; anyone who wishes to go into this side of the problem is referred to the writer's article 'Language and Immigration' in *Norwegian-American Historical Studies and Records,* X, 1-43 (1938). The perceptive reader will easily discover in the examples that follow the points of contact between the immigrants and the English-speaking world. The words borrowed were not necessarily for concepts new to the immigrants, though many of them were that also; but they were the words that most insistently met the immigrants as representatives of the social, political and economic world in which their new existence had its ultimate setting.

2.1 **Pure loanwords.** This is the largest single group of loans, consisting of 203 distinct words. These are divided according to parts of speech into 130 nouns, 6 pronouns, 16 adjectives, 5 numerals, 32 verbs, 11 adverbs, 2 prepositions, and 1 conjunction. It will be seen that no part of speech (except coincidentally the interjections) is entirely missing; but nouns are overwhelmingly in the majority, as usual in loanword lists, in part because of the predominance of nouns in the language.

2.2 **Loanword nouns.** These include 94 stems, 7 derivatives, and 29 compounds. Many of these are identified by accompanying articles or adjectives as either common or neuter gender, a distinction required by the structure of Dano-Norwegian for every noun. The appearance in these letters of the feminine gender (used in Norwegian speech for some loanwords) is extremely rare. Of those whose gender is positively identified in the letters 49 were common, 8 neuter; in the following list the rest have been classified according to the general usage in speech. Common gender is shown by the indefinite article *en* (or *ein*), adjectives not ending in *-t*, and the definite article *-en*, neuter gender by the indefinite article *et*, adjectives ending in *-t* and the definite article *-et*. The plural forms show a marked tendency toward importation of the English *-s*: common gender 12 *-s*, 5 *-er* (the usual Dano-Norwegian ending), 5 no ending (usual in Norwegian for words of measure, here including such words as *bushel, cent, rod*), 3 *-e* (words ending in *-r*), 3 *-ene* (definite plural); neuter gender 2 *-s*, 1 no ending (usual for Dano-Norwegian monosyllables, here *card*).

A. STEMS

1. Common Gender

Accident (ein forferdelig Aksident); *acre* (en 80 Akers farm; 4 busel Pr acer; 400 acre; det 80 acres Land stykke; 70 bushel Corn pr. acrs.; en 80 acre farm); *auto* (komme frem med Auto; Dem gaar i auto); *automobile* (den ene otomodillen efter den anden kom ind paa tunet); *barn* (Barns var kjørt ifra lange avstande); *barracks* (Sten for Soldats baraks); *bed* (fikse op vores Bed eller Bonke); *bill* (saa ikke alle Biller fryser i Komiten Hænder); *blizzard* (Wi har lidt koldt Veir sommetider men ingen Sne og ingen Blizard; Swedish: versta Blisert vi har hatt); *block* (bare 2 Blaks fra den norske Lutherske Kirke); *boss* (Vi fik da Kvelsmad og vær sin Økse av Bossen); *box* (vær dag var de Meget Pie ijen i boxen); *bus* (En "Chartered Bus" og mange biler; The Bus tar bare 8.00); *bushel* (100 Bushel Havre, 50 bush Hvede; nogle Busel med Havre; 4 busel Pr acer; Toogsækti pun i buslen); *business* (hans business var ikke fred).

Cake (kaffe og kek; Birthday cakes aa andre slags gaatter); *camp* (i Campene, i Campen, Stoven stod Mit i Mandscampen); *candy* (de tømte pailsful of candy til børnene); *canoe* (de havde canoes); *car* (en Car eller Radio; da car'en vilde fryse for os; Danish: hele Pladsen var fuld af Carre); *carnation* (en vakker bouquet af Carnation); *cemetery* (Frons Cemetary); *cent* (vorfor ikke Pute 2 sent in for Tomsen [Townsend]

THE IMPACT OF ENGLISH ON AMERICAN-NORWEGIAN LETTER WRITING

Plen); *check* (de må til byen hver fredag og faa sin check); *claim* (flytte til sin Claim); *class* (1st Class slædeføre); *clerk* (var deres [town board] cleark).

Dollar (to Daller; to dolar; 2 Daller; 2 Daler; 5-6 Dall; 8 dollars, 15 daller; 2 Daler); *dominion* (den som di andre provinser fik fra Dominion); *drive* (I skogen paa Driven og Sagmøllerne); *farm* (en 80 Akers farm; i by aa paa Farm; en Støre Farm; 2 Farme; Farmen; den gamle farm; Myhre-Farmen; Dem skal sette bo paa brudgomens faders farm); *feed* (Jeg kjøber Feed til dem... Feeden; bra med feed; saa fik vi nok til Kretura med Feed); *flax* (havre, byg og flax); *flood* (vi har ikke flood enda); *flour* (flour og flesk); *flu* (flu som raser al over; dødsaarsagen var Flu); *habit* (det er bleven en habit); *harvest* (arbeide i Harvisten); *husband* (min kjere husband, han var en trofast husban); *indian* (slaaes med Indiens); *interest* (herundt er det meste af interest the Roads); *island* (paa islan har vi ingen Snæ); *January* (Betalt I January); *job* (der fek han Job; jeg tog Joben); *jug* (saa Lars kan faa lidt paa Juggen; har han Juggen med).

Lease (maar du give Lease i det); *log* (Efter Nytaaret begynte dem at kjøre Logen ned til Elven); *lunch* (fattiman bakels, som ogsaa blev serveret me lunchen om aftenen); *molasses* (Kafe som de var megen Malases i); *money* (vis det ikke har blit spent moni); *Mrs.* (hos Mrs. Anne—); *navy* (gik ind i Navien, ifra Nevien); *nephew* (eleve nieces og nephew); *niece* (cf. preceding); *office* (Bossen havde sent et Brev ned til Offisen); *people* (dem er Red al pipel skal eta og drike sig ijel); *phone* (Budskab per Phone); *pie* (Jeg spiste Pie hele veien tilbage); *pioneer* (dem som kom Hær som Pionere); *plan* (Tomsen Plen); *pleurisy* (senere fik han Pluresie); *pony* (Indianerne satte dem op paa sine ponier); *practice* (Det har Jeg med Praktis fundet ut); *premier* (samelet med sinne Premier i Otava); *present* (du Kan Kjøbe pressent); *rack* (de baand som var igjen paa Ræcken); *radio* (en Car eller Radio); *relief* (nor en er poo Relif; Relifen er nok god at ta til; paa Releaf Arbeide; før folk fik Relief var det nok hyre hjelp at faa); *respects* (siste ære og respects); *river* (Paa Banken af midl rever); *road* (De var 8 Mand som arbeidet med Roadene; cf. *interest* above); *rod* (en 25 a 30 Rod øst ifra mit hus); *rutabaga* (Danish: Mais og Rudebagger).

Slough (nu er alt Landet under Plogen istedet [for] Sluer); *spot* (en krit vit spot); *stove* (fikse op Varmen i Stovene; det var nok hyggelig at vere runt stoven); *surprise* (de Siste 5 Uger har det veret Ligesom en Suprice at see); *tax* (for hai tæks); *thing* (alle slags gode tings at spise; dem fik Lidt Penge Ved siden af og som andre tings); *ticket* (sende Tiked; saa kjøber jeb ticket... "through ticket"); *track* (2 Mil fra Træken og til Campen; Swedish: ja har kipe træk); *trip* (kaame hid en trep, hun hade god Trep; en trip hjenem Min. S Dak og Iowa; at gjøre sinne trips); *turkey* (10 tusen tørkey, de tog os ud at se deres tørkey); *valley* (i denne

[83]

THE IMPACT OF ENGLISH ON AMERICAN-NORWEGIAN LETTER WRITING

Valley, rundt Valleyen); *yankee* (hun er yankee); *zero* (28 over zerow; under zerro; Swedish: 30-42 Blå Cero).

2. Neuter Gender

Card (Breve og Card); *college* (det var Studenterne fra Caleget, eftersom jeg forstod gik de alle paa Calege); *country* (Jeg liker Countryet og Climaet; det Beste som Kunde Rige op Contri og statene; Countryet og Omgivelserne og Climaet); *county* (I Jackson County; Eau Clari Kanty); *depot* (naar jeg kom til Hurley Wis, var min broder der paa Depoet); *duet* (et duet . . . blev sjunget; I hjemmet var der to duets); *load* (et durabelt load); *store* (der er et Store; da gik vi til et Store); *team* (med Teams); *town* 'township' (Town of Audobon; Taun of Vodside; I sit eget town; i vort Town of Hubbert; til Walvorth Taven); *train* (meget bedre for mig paa trainet).

B. DERIVATIVES

1. Common Gender

Assessor (I det borgerlige tjente han som Assessor; Assessor i mange Aar); *cookee* 'cook's helper' (Kokien. . .vilde da at jeg skulde blive Koken's hjelper eller Koki); *farmer* (En N Dak Farmer; vi er farmere; farmeren; farmerne); *gangster* (Gangsters og Græfters); *grafter* (cf. preceding); *hearing* (vor Første Hearing); *irrigation* (ingen irrigation i denne Valley); *living* (dem maa betale for leving baade til sig selv og andre); *morning* (ver morning); *revolver* (en Revolver); *settler* (alle setlere; En Sætler); *settling* (blev open for Setling); *subscription* (jeg sender ind en subskribsen for Decorah Posten); *vacation* (en lang vacation; deres Veketon; ellers havde de nok været tilbage fra sin Vækæsjen nu); *visitor* (mange visiters).

2. Neuter Gender

Allotment (det blev ikke noget af allotment endnu); *commissary* (Kommissary); *government* (Kasen va tom efter Tomley Guvementet); *granary* (det fylte jo ikke meget i Grenereet); *grocery* (saa faar jo alle Grossery verd 8 dollars; med al Post og grocerier); *settlement* (de grundla Lake Hendricks settlementet; i Kristiania Settlement); *township* (Stoni chreck township; gamel Pioner fra Walwort Tounship).

C. COMPOUNDS

Aeroplane (vis at jeg kan faa Decora Postens Arow Plan); *birthday cake* (mange Birthday cakes aa andre slags gaatter); *brick building* (børnene blev stuvede ind i en brickbuilding); *chicken dinner* (at spise "chicken dinner"); *cloud burst* (Swedish: den 15 Juni hade vi klad

THE IMPACT OF ENGLISH ON AMERICAN-NORWEGIAN LETTER WRITING

Börst); *community hall* (en Korsvei over denne hvor der er et Store, en "Community Hall" og nogle Huse); *county attorney* (Han var County Attorney i flere terminer); *county seat* (I vores county seat); *coupling pole* (en som var kommet sig under vognboxen og hængt sig fast i coupling polen); *drayman* (han har vert dri man I fargo); *grandchildren* (og saa har han 3 Grænkjilderen); *homestead* (tog Homstet; her fik dem Land paa Homsted; provet op Homsted; min Homsted; min Svoger havde taget Homestead); *homestead land* (alle toge da Homestead Land); *life sketch* (Mr og Mrs Bergs Life Sketch forfattet og læst av Mr Halsvick); *middling biscuit* (saam Levede hele Vinteren Paa Bare Midling Bisketer og Vand); *money order* (money order for $2.50; Postmony Ordres); *notary public* (Notari Public); *office cleaning* (har havt mange slags Arbeide...Offis Klining); *ore transport* (daarlig Oretransport); *pailful* (cf. *candy* above); *pallbearer* (Pallbearers var...; Pallbereren's Navne var...); *picnic supper* (saa havde vi picknick souper og en hyggelig aften); *pioneer settler* (pioneer Setlere af denne Egn); *postmaster* (Koloniets "Postmaster"); *Prime minister* (Premiminister Benet).

Railroad (vi jik efter Railroaden i 33 Mil); *sidewalk* (de var saa Varmt paa Saidvalken); *state fair* (sidste høst paa Oregons Statefare); *strawhat* (han kjøpte en Strawhat); *thanksgiving* (Swedish: tänksgivneng var versta Blisert vi har hatt); *toastmaster* (Vi havde med os Rev. G. W. Mathne som Toastmaster); *toploader* (skulde blive Toploader); *town clerk* ("Town Clerk"); *train service* (vi har haft tran sirvis ganske regular); *violin selection* (Mr. Wallers Violin Selection var smuk); *war veteran* (en War-veteran fra Borgerkrigen); *wedding cake* (havde med sig en vakker wedding cake).

D. PHRASES

These are usually unit expressions naming some institution or company: *Co-operative Elevator Co., Dexter Insurance Co.;* or some longer title of a position: *Justice of Peace, Sunday School Teacher, Government Census Collector,* etc.

2.3 **Loanword pronouns.** As a class pronouns are of such high frequency that they are not easily displaced by loanwords. The following examples have been found, all in letters showing generally limited writing ability: *I, him* (ei naa det er mange som naa him); *this* (Takker saa hjertelig faar des Papir); *what* (vot de siger er sant); *some* (Jeg haaber som Vefsen Væring laeser Decorah Posten; det var faagi og kalt og bles ta øst og det snøga som ogsaa; give some af de Unge Paintion); *something* (naar saa tankerne komer i arbeide finer man somting man aldri har rigti forstaaet).

2.4 Loanword adjectives. Like the nouns they can be divided into stems, derivatives, and compounds. The Norwegian suffixes showing the gender and number of accompanying nouns are seldom used, and are here limited to stems: *-t* neuter, *-e* plural.

A. STEMS

Great (et gret vede Distrigt); *model* (en model farm); *plenty* (plenty sne); *slow* (Lomverringerne var for Sloe); *solid* (paa salled grund); *tough* (hær runt Clearbrook har de inte været saa taaf læl).

B. DERIVATIVES

Suffix *-y*: *Foggy* (det var faagi og kalt og bles ta øst) *sorry* (jeg er saarig for at jeg. . . har blevet Behind); suffix *-ed, -t*: *blocked* (Danish: vejen har været blokket); *blockaded* (Banen havde været blocadet fra Willmar west; veiene har været Blakeda mange Steds); *bothered* (Wi behøver ikke at Blive badret med den Tanke); *chartered* (En "Chartered Bus"); *informed* (jeg er informed at. . .); *lost* (vil blive Lost).

C. COMPOUNDS

Lifelong (en af de beste Lifelong Kammerater); *second-handed* (ligemeget om det er brugt eller Second Handed).

2.5 Loanword numerals. These are seldom borrowed (though the writer has heard the use of E numerals in certain communities). The following occur: *forty* (slik kulde har vi nok aldrig haft i fra forty til fem og femty); occasionally in dates, e.g. *1st, 26th, 29th;* *one* (Posten er von of de best blade i Amerik).

2.6 Loanword adverbs. None of the examples here found were derived from adjectives, so that there was no occasion to apply the N suffix *-t*: *abreast* (gade op og gade ned, 2-3 brest); *all right* (alt syntes at gaa alright); *also* (jeg har alsaa tilbragt 4 aar paa Melbo; skal also hilse [context makes clear that these are not the N altsaa]; *away* (at dem ikke skule faa lov at giv vei noget

THE IMPACT OF ENGLISH ON AMERICAN-NORWEGIAN LETTER WRITING

... kjøbe pressent og sende vei); *before* (vores navn var Henry Quale before); *behind* (cf. *sorry* above); *even* (Even mange Prester tro bare paa Penge Pungen); *fifty-fifty* (hvorfor ikke gaa 50-50, saa vilde Mangt blive Anderledes); *regular* (vi har haft tran sirvis ganske regular); *through* (Naar det gaar tru, da er det tisnok at bekymmere sig); *where* (vær han Havde sit Hjæm; Hver har det blivet af Ola og Per).

2.7 Loanword verbs. Only stems occur among the borrowed verbs. In a few cases E inflections were imported, but usually the N inflections were substituted: inf. -*e*, pret. -*ede* or -*te* (speech forms: -*e*, -*a*, -*et*), p.p. -*et* or -*t* (-*e*, -*a*). *Board* (han bordede en tid hos min broder); *celebrate* (da hu celebrete sin 90 aars fødselsdag); *commit* (hvad de haver committed); *cripple* (til at kryple op og skyde ned en milion eller 2); *cure* (det er om og jøre om han kan kure det); *declare* (da Nye declared at de vilde have brug for $7000); *depend* (vi kan depende paa Avling); *dig* (mange tak til alle som var med og dige grava); *farm* (De farmet sit land her til i nittiaarene; dem som Farmer nu; bgynte Farme); *feed* (ut av 100 som Jeg har fide en a to gange daglig); *fix* (fikse op Varmen i Stovene; fikse op vores Bed eller Bonke; det er længe siden du Fixet op mit kjøkken).

Happen (heppenet til at vere runt her); *hitch* (jeg hitched oxerne til slæden...jeg hitchet dem til vognen); *hunt* (jeg har Huntet Runt at faa flere Abomet [Abonnenter]); *keep* (Swedish: ja har kipe træk Ock skrive ned i en spesel Bok); *know* (ei naa det er mange som naa him); *load* (dem kunde loade paa et durabelt load); *make* (jeg skulde meket en god moro); *notice* (om vi ikke notis det); *operate* (opering en fylling station); *pave* (den som Paved veien for ham); *pay* (saa sliper dem at pei dem); *phone* (Swedish: Ja fåna till mina Nabor); *pitch* (hun maate pitche paa stakken); *prove* (provet op Homsted); *put* (vorfor ikke Pute 2 sent in for Tomsen Plen; wil dere putte disse or ind i decoraposten; at pute de i avisen); *rent* (dem har Rænte et Pent Hus); *rig* (det Beste som Kunde Rige op Contri og statene); *save* (Jorde alt Som Stod i Dems Magt faarat Saive ham); *settle* (Flytede saa op Til Winger Minnesota Hvor dem Sætlede ned; Setla ned i Nerheden; setlede ned paa Land 9 Miles fra Byen Bottineau); *visit* (ogsaa visite [pret.] vi Julijus og Otilde Hælgesen); *vote* (Vaagn op og vote for deres Ret; Vote for mig, du Ola).

2.8 **Loanword conjunctions and prepositions.** These classes are very sparsely represented: *and* (Mr end Mrs; Mr en Mrs, Harry en Engebret Soland; her en der); *below* (28 Belo; Swedish: 30-42 Blå Cero, belå Cero); *past* (Nu er jeg Past 75 aar).

3.1 **Loanword spellings.** As the reader will have noticed, the imported E morphemes are often spelled in a markedly Norwegian way. This is in itself evidence that many of them have been thoroughly absorbed into the language. Of course it is only the writers with relatively little English schooling who commit these 'errors'; they reflect their own pronunciations in the spelling which they reconstruct, at least in part, according to N rules. Correct English spellings tell us nothing about the pronunciations and have therefore not been included in the list below; but most of the incorrect ones do. By reading across the columns one can see how these spellings have come into being: in column 1 the English pronunciation is shown in IPA transcription, in 2 the English spelling; in 3 is given the AmN (mis-)spelling and in 4 the AmN pronunciation which it probably represents; in the last column examples are given (which are not complete for all sounds). Among the examples are included some of the proper names found in the letters.

THE IMPACT OF ENGLISH ON AMERICAN-NORWEGIAN LETTER WRITING

A. Vowels

AmE sound	Eng. spellings	AmN respellings	AmN sound	Examples
[i]	e, ea, ee, eo, ie, y	i, ea, ie, ig	i	Cl*i*vland, Tot*i*msteren, kl*i*ning, s*i*d, f*i*de, k*i*pe, kok*i*, p*i*pel, rel*i*f, rel*ea*f, notar*i*, pon*i*er, faag*i*, contr*i*, Ston*i* Chreck, Ragb*i*, Rappit Chit*i*, plures*i*e, saar*ig*.
[ɪ]	i, ee	(1)e	e	l*e*ving, tr*e*p, sall*e*d, Ston*i* Chr*e*ck, Min*e*aples
	ee, e	(2)i	i	Franskr*i*k, harv*i*sten
[eɪ]	a, ea, ai, ay	(1)e	e	n*e*vien, k*e*k, m*e*ket, vek*e*t[i]on, G*e*lsvile, Norv*e* Lake
		(2)ei, ai, i	ei	p*ei*, v*ei* (away), m*ai*sen, s*ai*ve, dr*i* man
		(3)æ	æ	væk*æ*sjen
[ɛ]	e, ea	(1)e	e	i br*e*st
		(2)æ	æ	r*æ*nte, s*æ*tlede
		(3)a	æ?	Pl*a*sant Ridge, Pl*a*sent Valy
	e, ea, ai (before r)	(4)æ, e, a	æ	stat*e*fare, v*æ*r (where), hv*e*r, cemet*a*ry, pallbereren
[æ]	a	(1)e	e	t*e*x, gr*e*nereet, h*e*ppenet, Mant*e*ne (Montana), B*e*lfour
		(2)æ	æ	gr*æ*fters, gr*æ*nkjilderen, tr*æ*ken, Gr*æ*n Forks, Gr*æ*ften (Grafton), träk (Swedish), t*æ*ks, tänksgivneng (Swedish)
[ə]	a, ui, ai, o	æ, e	ə	v*æ*kæsjen, Indi*e*ns, *e*n (and), vek*e*t[i]on, Pl*a*sent Valy, Mant*e*ne, bisk*e*ter, Mount*e*n, m*ai*sen, Gr*æ*ften
[əl]	le	el	əl	pip*el*, baycick*el*
[ər]	or, re, er, ur	er, ir, ør, ear	ər, ?ør	visit*er*s, ak*er*s, fei*er*mand, s*ir*vis, t*ør*key, cl*ear*k, klad Börst
[a]	o, au	a	a	bl*a*ks, bl*a*keda, b*a*dret, b*a*dra, c*a*lege, d*a*ller, d*a*ler, s*a*lled, M*a*ntene, *a*ttomobil

[89]

THE IMPACT OF ENGLISH ON AMERICAN-NORWEGIAN LETTER WRITING

AmE sound	Eng. spellings	AmN respellings	AmN sound	Examples
[aɪ]	i	(1) ei	ei	*ei* (I), f*ei*ermand
		(2) ai, ay	ai	s*ai*dvalken, b*ay*cickel
[aʊ]	ou, ow	(1) a	a	k*a*nty, kl*a*d Börst
		(2) au, ou, ave	æu	t*ou*nship, t*av*en, Watert*ou*n
[ɔ]	a, o	aa	å	Fergus F*aa*ls, f*aa*gi, s*aa*rig
[ʊ]	oo	o	o	k*o*ki, V*o*dside
	eu, ou	u	u	pl*u*resie, Miss*u*ri
[oʊ]	o, oa, ow, oo	o, ow	o	Okland, zer*ow*, sl*o*e, bel*o*, R*o*svelt, R*o*swelth, Ar*ow* Plan, b*o*rdede
		å, aa	å	n*aa* (know), Swed. f*å*na, bel*å*
[ʌ]	u, ou	(1) aa	å	t*aa*f
		(2) o	o	b*o*nke (bunk), c*o*ntri
		(3) a	a	R*a*gbi
		(4) u	u	g*u*vementet
[u]	ough, oo	(1) u	u	tr*u*, sl*u*er
		(2) o	o	Liverp*o*l, Liver P*o*ll

B. Consonants

[p]	p	pp	pp	Ra*pp*it Chiti
[t]	t, tt	(1) tt	tt	a*tt*omobil
		(2) th	t	Nordako*th*a, Roswel*th*
[θ]	th	t	t	som*t*ing, *t*ings, *t*ru, Walwor*t*
[ð]	th	d	d	ba*d*ret, ba*d*ra
[k]	c, ck	k, c, ck, ch	k	pic*k*nic*k*, baycic*k*el, Stoni Chrec*k*, *k*ek, *k*ure, *k*omissary, *k*anty, *k*oki, a*k*ers, Frans*k*rik, De*k*ora, blo*c*adet, træ*k*en, ti*k*ed, bara*k*s, bri*k*, bla*k*s, etc.
[ks]	x	ks	ks	fi*ks*e, a*ks*ident, tæ*ks*
[g]	g	(1) gg	gg	ju*gg*en
	gg	(2) g	g	faa*g*i
[f]	gh	f	f	taa*f*
[v]	v	w	v	Ros*w*elth

THE IMPACT OF ENGLISH ON AMERICAN-NORWEGIAN LETTER WRITING

AmE sound	Eng. spellings	AmN respellings	AmN sound	Examples
[w]	w	v	v	*v*ei (away), said*v*alken, *v*on (one)
[hw]	wh	v, hv	v	*v*ær, h*v*er, *v*ot (what)
[tʃ]	ch	kj	(t)ç	grænk*j*ilderen
[dð]	dg	dj	dj	Do*dj*e
[j]	(u)	j	j	*J*ulen (Ulen)
[z]	s	(1)c	s	sup*r*ice
		(2)ss	ss	pre*ss*ent
[s]	c	(1)s	s	offi*s*en, *s*ent, sirvi*s*
		(2)ss	ss	gro*ss*ery
[ʃ]	sh, ti	(1)s	s	bu*s*el, bu*s*len, Ru*s*ford, subskrib*s*en
		(2)sj	ʃ	vækæ*sj*en
[l]	l	(1)ll	ll	sa*ll*ed (solid)
	ll	(2)l	l	ca*l*ege, Pleasant Va*l*ey, Tvin Va*l*e
[n]	nn	(1)n	n	Mi*n*eaples
	n	(2)nn	nn	ja*nn*itor arbeide
[r]	rr	r	r	saa*r*ig

C. Silent Letters

| O | i, e, o, u | O | O | Villston (Williston), kek, von (one), somting, praktis, La Cros, Camros, som (some), offis, sirvis, Minneaplais, Minneaples, Audbon |
| O | t, d, k, r | O | O | depoet (depo+def. art.), islan, husban, Græn Forks, naa (know), suprice |

3.2 **Interpretation.** The misspellings of English words reflect rather clearly the typical substitutions of Norwegian sounds for the English ones.

1) Of the English vowels only [i], [a], [ɔ], and [ə] are consistently reproduced by a single Norwegian sound, reasonably close to the English. The rest show vacillation between two or more Norwegian sounds, none

[91]

of which is precisely equivalent to the English: [ɪ]>N i, e; [oʊ]>N o, å; [u]>N u, o; [ʌ]>N å, o, a, u; [æ]>N e, æ; [ɛ]>N e, æ; [aɪ]> N ei, ai; [aʊ]>N a, æu.

2) The English consonants are more consistently reproduced by single equivalents. After short vowels there is a clear tendency to double and lengthen the consonants, while after long vowels they are often simplified: a*tt*omobil vs. faa*g*i. Certain English consonants are entirely lacking in N, and for these N substitutes nearby sounds. These are: [hw] and [w]>v; [θ]>t; [ð]>d; [z]>s; [tʃ]>ç (spelled kj); [dʒ]>dj. The substitution of s for [ʃ] is a limited dialectal phenomenon in such words as *bushel*.

3) The numerous alternatives of English spelling often led to confusion, showing that the writer knew the pronunciation but was uncertain of the spelling—e.g., picknick, releaf, saive, valy, zerow. In other cases the misspellings were more phonetic than the English: x>ks, ck>k, gh>f, ie>i. Similarly with the loss of silent letters; in some cases these reveal common folk pronunciations, e.g. Græn Forks.

4.1 Loanblends. If any single part of the loanword has been altered to make way for a native morpheme, it may be regarded as a loanblend. Some of the words listed above (2.2) among the loanword derivatives often appear in speech as loanblends, e.g. *farmer* which is pronounced *farmar* in some dialects, with substitution of the Norwegian morpheme of agency *-ar*. But in written Dano-Norwegian there is complete coincidence of the English and the Norwegian suffixes. The noun suffixes belonging to this group are *-er*, *-ing*, *-ment*, and *-ery*; the examples are listed above, under loanword derivatives. Those which show an adaptation to Norwegian spelling habits are *subskripsen*, *vækæsjen*, and *groceri*; in addition, there is grammatical adaptation of *farmere* 'farmers,' *setlere* 'settlers,' *guvementet* 'the government,' *settlementet* 'the settlement,' and *grocerier* 'groceries.' The adjective suffixes belonging here are *-y*, *-ed*, and *-t*; those words which show spelling or grammatical adaptation are *saarig* 'sorry,' *blokket* 'blocked,' *blakeda* 'blockaded,' and *badret* 'bothered.' Only in one case do we have a clear-cut instance of a loanblend derivative: *solicitere* 'solicit' with substitution of the N *-ere* (han soliciterte Subskribenter for Bladet). The apparently parallel

THE IMPACT OF ENGLISH ON AMERICAN-NORWEGIAN LETTER WRITING

visitere 'visit' may be a loanshift extension, though the Norwegian word is rare.

4.2 Loanblend compounds. These are rather common, constituting as they do about one half of the whole number of compounds. A few of those listed as loanwords above (2.2) would probably have to be classified as loanblends in speech, but spelling does not permit us to make a distinction from the English morpheme: dri *man* 'drayman,' Ore*transport, post*master, premi*minister* 'prime minister,' Homestead *Land,* Straw*hat, Top*loader, *Violin* Selection. The unquestionable loanblend compounds can be distinguished into NUCLEAR and MARGINAL; the nuclear are those in which the nucleus or last element is imported, the marginal those in which the first element is imported.

1. MARGINAL

(1) Common Gender: *bicycle cap* (en Baycickel hue); *brick builder* (Brik bygere); *cement road* (Det er 6 mil til den Cementveien); *coat pocket* (han havde $250.00 i sin Coat lome); *common school* (Holt nu Common Skole nogle Aar); *fireman* (er gift med en Feiermand); *policeman* (Saa dum som han da var at han ikke gjik til en Police Mand); (2) Neuter Gender: *courthouse* (Jeg og min Mand Sad paa Court Huset en hel dag); *farm home* (i sit Farm-hjem); *feed loan, seed loan* (Farmerne har maatet haft baade Sid Laan og Feed Laan); *janitor work* (Jannitor arbeide); *legislative work* (merre Legislatur arbeide fra Minnesota); *masonry work* (alt Slags Maisen arbeide).

2. NUCLEAR

(1) Common gender: *ammunition magnate* (en amusjonsmagnet); *sales tax* (at Betalle Omsetnings Tex; vi betaler nok omsetnings-tæks); *straw pile* (en en og to års gamell strå Pile; stra Pile); *two-teamster* (Totimsteren sagde at . . .); *wagon box* (en som var kommet sig under vognboxen); *war veteran* (han var en krigs veteran); (2) neuter gender: *Christmas card* (tak. . . for Jule Card); *ox team* (mursten var Kjørt ind med Oxeteam); *ox yoke* (et par oxer og et oxeyoke).

5.1 Loanshifts. The test of a loanshift is that it consists entirely of native morphemes. It is here assumed that any word known to have occurred in the Norwegian language before 1880 is native from the point of view of American Norwegian. The loanshift may be a single word, a derivative, a compound, a phrase, or a construction; if only the meaning is new, it is an extension, otherwise it is a novation.

5.2 **Extensions.** In the writer's article in *Language*, cited above, a distinction was made between loan synonyms and homonyms, according to whether the new and the old meanings had anything in common. A more satisfactory classification can be based on the other terms there suggested, viz. homologue, homophone, and analogue. When the native and the borrowed usage of a word have nothing but a semantic contact, as when American Portuguese *frio* 'a cold spell' comes to mean 'a cold infection,' the extension is SYNONYMOUS. When the usages have nothing but a phonetic contact, as when AmN *fil* 'file' comes to mean 'field,' the extension is HOMOPHONOUS. In most cases there is both a semantic and a phonetic similarity, as when AmN *korn* 'grain' comes to mean 'Indian corn,' and then we may call the extension HOMOLOGOUS. There are no synonymous extensions in the material here being analyzed; there are very few in AmN in general. In the following list the native Norwegian meaning is given first, then the new meaning found in AmN. A practical test of the distinction between the homologous and the homophonous extension is that the former might appear in a dictionary as an additional meaning of the word, while the latter would require a new entry. But this would apply only in a dictionary which entirely disregarded etymology in its arrangement of definitions.

A. Homologous Extensions

1. Stems

Nouns: *grøn* 'cereal food' > 'grain' (alle sorter Grøn; noge Lund med Grøn); *hyre* 'employment at sea' > 'employment' from English *hire* (fik hyre i Skogen for et Sag møle Co.); *korn* 'grain' > 'maize' (dit Corn; flax og corn); *likør* 'sweet alcoholic drink' > 'liquor' (Likørsalget); *mil* 'ab. 11

THE IMPACT OF ENGLISH ON AMERICAN-NORWEGIAN LETTER WRITING

km.' > 'ab. 1.6 km.' (2 Mil; 9 Miles fra Byen); *papir* 'paper' > 'newspaper' (jeg saa i Papiret; i hjenem deres Paper; Takker saa hjertelig faar des Papir; han har hold eders papir; faar nu papiret til dens tid er oppe); *plads* 'tenant farm,' 'room' > 'large farm,' 'place' (vi har alle Slags forretnigs Plaser; Decorah—det burde vere en God Plads; paa same Plads; Byen Lacrosse er en fin liden Plas; somme plasser Rundt her; fra saa mange Plaser; ingen plas paa jorden; men jeg seer de har Blizard andre Pladser); *provins* 'province' > 'Canadian province' (vor provins); *ton* 'ship's ton' > 'American ton' (faa et halt tøn om gangen); *vei* 'path, road' > 'way, manner' (den vei verden er nu; denne vei døde han).

Adjectives: *mest* 'most' (greatest quantity) > 'most' (greatest number) (i de meste hjem); *tro* 'faithful' > 'real' (han var en tro mand).

Adverbs: *rett* 'straight' > 'right' (det er rett i byen vi lever).

Verbs: *gaa* 'walk' > 'go' (vi kan da gaa til Døllalaget i Sommer; ser Dem gaar i auto opijenem Prestberget; saa solgte jeg mit Hus og jik til Amerika; Wi gik fra Christiania den 16 Mai 1884); *lede* 'guide' > 'lead, as a road,' for the correct N *føre* (en militær Vei... leder igjennom denne Bygd); *leve* 'be alive' > 'dwell, live' (levede syd fra Hans Ruen; found in 22 writers); *mene* 'have the opinion, intend to say' > 'signify, mean' (det mener saa meget); *række* 'extend, stretch out' > 'attain' (derfor rækker hun den høie alder); *stoppe* 'pause' > 'stay, dwell' (han stoppede hos Ole Elstad; jeg stop høs Knut Benson; stopede; staappe dær en uge; for at staape over natten; staapper me hende; har stopet hos mig de 4 siste vintre).

2. Derivatives

Adjectives: *ængstelig* 'worried' > 'eager' from Eng. *anxious* (Han var ængstelig for kirkens velfærd og fremgang).

Verbs: *lande* 'land after a sea voyage' > 'arrive at a destination' from Eng. *land* (Vi landet i Yankton); *moderere* 'moderate' trans. > intrans. (kulden har moderert en del).

3. Compounds

Nouns: *hjemsted* 'native place' > 'homestead,' a technical term in landownership (de tog sig et hjemsted); *nykommer* 'a recent arrival' > 'a recent arrival in America, a greenhorn' (da Jeg som nykommer gik til Fots 10 mil ind til Fosston i 50 under zerro).

B. Homophonous Extensions

1. Stems

Nouns: *bank* 'bank, a financial institution' > 'bank of a river' (Paa Banken af midl rever); *fil* 'file' > 'field' (meget arbede er jort paa filen; det ser ud til at vi kan snart til i fila); *lot* 'share in fishing expedition' > 'lot for house' (Men saa kjøbte han sig Hus aa laat; en lot av den gamle farm); *magazin* '(military) storehouse'>'periodical' (Magaciner); *parti* 'political party'>'social party' (det blev et parti for helle Nilse Slækten; Stort Æresparti for Rev. O. J. Hagen); *rest* 'remainder'>'rest from one's work' (en god Rest).

Verbs: *reise* 'lift up, erect'>'rear, bring up' (da jeg er reist paa gaarden Rusnes i Vaage; jeg var inte Netop raisa op iblant Storbønderne); *spænde* 'kick'>'spend' (spende tiden; de $125,000 de havde spent; vor jeg spænte mine lit over 30 Aar; spente pengene; vis det ikke har blit spent moni paa forselige ting).

Adverbs: *oppe* 'up'>'gone, over' from E *up* (faar nu papiret til dens tid er oppe).

Interjections: *vel* 'good'>'well' interjection (vell. jeg vill ei sende mere denne gang; well vi faar jo nu snart høre og se vordan det blir).

2. PHRASES

Nominal: *god tid* 'plenty of time'>'enjoyable time' (Vi hadde god tid om Vinteren Skaitø over Otta).

Verbal: *se op* 'look up'>'show up' (vad tid skal Ola og Per se op igjen i Bladet); *tage ind* 'take in' (literally)>'attend a meeting' (Jeg har inte Tat ind mer en et Lag Siden Torekven Blev borte).

5.3 **Loanshift creations.** These are found wherever novel expressions have come into being by the rearrangement of native morphemes. It is possible, with Werner Betz in his excellent study of the Old High German loans from Latin, *Deutsch und Lateinisch* (Bonn, 1949), to divide these into literal (Lehnübersetzung) and approximate (Lehnübertragung) reproductions of the foreign model. He even adds a third variety, the Lehnschöpfung, in which there is no morphemic similarity to the foreign model; these might be called 'induced creations' and united with the 'hybrid creations' discussed in the writer's article. These two types of creation would then form a class of words coming into being in one language through influence from another, but not formally modeled upon the expression in the other language. No further analysis of the loanshift creations will here be attempted, since their number is small, and they are mostly literal imitations of the kind usually known as 'loan translations.' Included here are not only derivatives and compounds, but also phrases and

THE IMPACT OF ENGLISH ON AMERICAN-NORWEGIAN LETTER WRITING

constructions. The distinction between the two latter is one between specific expressions, such as 'pay up,' here called phrases, and generalized expressions, chiefly syntactic relationships, here called constructions.

A. DERIVATIVES

Verb: *plane* 'plan' [from Norwegian *plan* 'a plan' and the verbal suffix -e] (kommer ingen vei med noget af havd dem bestemer og Planer).

B. COMPOUNDS

Nouns: *fyllingstation* 'filling station' (opering en fylling station); *hjempladsen* 'the home place' (Emil er Paa Jempladsen); *hyrehjælp* 'hired help' (før folk fik Relief var det nok hyre hjelp at faa). Two awkward attempts to create Norwegian compounds from English concepts are exceptional: *gamle-aldersvaghed* 'old age weakness' (dode aaf Gamle-alder svaghed); *sengefasthed* 'being bedfast' (avgik ved døden efter næsten fem måneders sengefasthed).

C. PHRASES

Adverbial: *al over* 'all over' (all over det ganske Land; flu som raser al over; vor dem er alover); *alt rundt* 'all round' (Veildyrkede Farmme alt ront); *ud af orden* 'out of order' (det vilde ikke være ud af orden ved ovennævnte anledninger at give den Norsk-Amerikanske presse den plads den fortjener); *vel af* 'well off' (vi er vel af, vi har ikke flood enda).

Verbal: *betale op* 'pay up' (betaldt op for Bladet); *er...paa* 'is (going) on' (det er jo ingen slags krig paa); *have til at* 'have to' (vi har til at være punktlig med betalingen); *kjøbe ud* 'buy out' (til dere Kjøbte den ud); *sne ind* 'snow in' (Decorah er blet sneet ind); *sælge ud* 'sell out' (var en kort tid paa farmen igjen men solgte i 1898 ud og flyttet til Folton).

D. CONSTRUCTIONS

Norwegian word order has given way to English in the following cases, resulting in new constructions: (1) subject/verb instead of verb/subject after a part of the predicate: og derfor *jeg ønsker* at have det. (2) Adverb/verb instead of verb/adverb in main clause: han ligte posten meget godt og *altid ventet* med glæde paa den; en søster og 3 brødre *ogsaa begræder* hans død. (3) Verb/adverb instead of adverb/verb in subordinate clause: som *havde alt ved denne Tid* levet her henimod 20 Aar; at hans venner og kjendte... *kunde ogsaa* faa at kjende om ham; da vi *har inte* langt efter; somting man aldri *har rigti* forstaaet. (4) Month/ordinal

[97]

instead of ordinal/month in dates: Marts den tolvte, aprild 3die, Aug 17, Mars 26, Mai 1ste, dec. 23. (5) Preposition/noun instead of noun/preposition: *over natten* 'over night' (two writers). (6) Reversing order of adverbs in phrases of location: *oppe der* 'up there' (Norw. deroppe); *runt her* 'around here' (three writers).

5.4 **Doubtful cases.** The problem of identification has been discussed by the writer in the article cited above, pp. 226-30. The following examples include words used very much as in English, but they cannot be positively identified as loans since the words also occurred in the Dano-Norwegian of the immigrants: *chance* (give Kvinderne Chance til at styre); *fort* (naar dette Fort blev anlagt i 1864); *guitar* (Gettar); *ideal* (en Ideal Personlighed); *mine* (Minen; Jærnminen); *parliament* (parlamentet); *pension* (give some af de Unge Paintion); *point* (fra denne historiske punkt i Norge [viz. Eidsvold]; *region* (bebode denne region). The following examples also have a suspiciously English ring, but can be attested from some dialects: *indkomme* 'income' (det er mange aar uden inkome; cf. Aasen *Norsk Ordbog*); *part* 'part' (den siste Part af September); *prente* 'print' (Eftther som jeg ei saag mitt sistte Brev Prentted i D. Postten); *skøite* 'skate' (da han Skjøitet over Otta; cf. *Norsk Riksmåls-Ordbok*); *under* 'below' (det var 10 under 0).

The forms *svigersøster* 'sister-in-law' and *svigerbarn* 'children-in-law' were formed on the analogy of *svigerfar* 'father-in-law' and similar N forms; it is hard to say whether the E words might not also have played a part by their obvious parallelism. The usage found in one letter of *efterleve* for 'survive' may be an induced creation from Norwegian *efterlevende* 'survivor' (two Døtre efter lever hende); but *forekomme* 'grant' is an older Dano-Norwegian usage (saa snild at forekomme mit Ønske).

6.1 **Conclusions.** Our analysis of the impact of English on the letters of Norwegian immigrants of fifty or more years of residence in America shows that the chief influence is one of numerous loanwords for the phenomena of American life. These include stems, derivatives, compounds, and phrases; of the compounds about one-half show partial morphemic substitution, and are therefore called loanblends. Many of the English expressions thus adopted are respelled in such a way as to reflect the pronunciation given them by the AmN speakers; a number of the vowels show marked vacillation as to which Norwegian sound should properly be substituted for the English ones. The only English inflection which is introduced with the loanwords is the plural in *-s*; about one-half of the loan nouns occurring in the plural show this, while the rest have Norwegian plurals. A number of examples were found of loanshifts, particularly extensions of meaning, in which native expressions acquired new meanings because of their similarity to foreign expressions either in sound or in sound and meaning. In a very small number of cases there were actual novations in the language which had been produced by a slavish imitation of English expressions for which native morphemes were substituted.

7.1 Texts. The three passages that follow are examples of the language and subject matter found in many of the letters examined. The first passage is selected from a longer letter; the second and third are complete letters. No change in spelling has been made except to italicize the English loans. The spelling in these samples is poorer than the average; they have been chosen to illustrate loanword usage.

(1) *Reminiscences from a Wisconsin Lumber Camp*

[Minneapolis, Minnesota]

De var ikke svært stor *Camp* 40 mand i alt, De var 8 Mand som arbeidet med *Roadene* og dem havde ganske langt at gaa og jeg Maate bære Midag ud til dem Jeg havde en *box* paa rygen og en *Tekande* at bære og jeg kokte *Teen* ude i Skogen og vær dag var de Meget *Pie* ijen i *boxen* Jeg spiste *Pie* hele veien tilbage til *Campen,* Efter Nyt aaret begynte dem at kjøre *Logen* ned til Elven paa dise store Slæder dem kunde *loade* paa et durabelt *Load* paa dem, Stort som et Hus. De var en Franskmand som kom og skulde blive *Toploader* og naar han havde omtrent en *Mil* ijen at gaa til *Campen* om kvelden da fik han se en stor flaak Med Ulve kome efter sig og han maate da klyve op i et Træ og sate sin Sæk med Klæder i Nede Ved Træt og Ulvene kom og rev hans Sæk i biter og hans Klæder spret udover i Sneen og han maate side der i Træet hele Naten og paa Morgenen kom han til *Campen* og var næsten ijælfrøset han sagde at de var den længste og hordeste Nat i sit liv, Vi havde en Udmerket *Boss* han var Irlænder og jeg likte mig gaat der, Vist at dete komer i Posten skal jeg skrive mere siden og Mere Intresant, og saa til sist en Vænlig hilsen til Posten's læsere og dets Redaktør og Pærsonale i fra Mig som ogsaa ær fød paa den Naturskjøne Ø, Ytterøen Norge.

(2) *Renewal of Subscription*

[Ettrick, Wisconsin]

Ja naar Jeg ser paa Adresse Lappen paa Bladet saa ser Jeg at Jeg Lesser paa Credit da det skulde veret Betalt I *January* men det blev Overset paa Grund af at Jeg ikke Var Hjemme den Siste Maaned, og da faar Jeg herved sende *Tiked* saa Posten Kan faa *Visitere* os et Aar til da Jeg liker at Lesse nu i Disse Kaalde og Stormfulde dage. Ja dette maa vere hvad vore Forfedre Kalder Gamle dags Vinter thi det Snoger og Blaaser en dag og Blaaser og Sner den Anden, og Spretende Kaalt saa det ser ud som Kviksølvet har froset fast under Null thi de Siste 5 Uger har det veret Ligesom en *Suprice* at see det ovenfor saa Sant at Sigge saa har dette veret en Haard vinter med meget Sne og Kulde og Sneplogerne er i fult sving baade Nat og Dag. Saa disse mend som skal prøve at faa Posten og Andet Lesse stof Runt til *Farmerne* faar Sinne Hender fulde for at gjøre sinne *trips* Med beste Hilsener til Posten og dens mange Lessere.

(3) *Friendly Gossip*

[Clearbrook, Minnesota]

vi har naak hat en gammel dags vinter i vinter, me kulde aa sne, men hær runt Clearbrook har de inte været saa *taaf* læl da vi *har inte* langt efter alslags ve. saa de ville være vaar egen sjyld om vi stælte aas slik at vi maate fryse. di 2 første maaner of dette aar har været meget lange saa de var en hygge, vær dag Decorah Posten Kom. thi da kan vi læse mange interesante breve fra alle kanter. den 31 Jan var der mange *visiters* hos Mrs Anne—da hu *celebrete* sin 90 aars fødselsdag. hu modtog mange lykønskninger baade i form af breve aa gaver, aa saa mange *Birthday cakes* aa andre slags gaatter, selv hadde hu bagt fattiman bakels, som ogsaa blev serveret me *lunchen* om aftenen. hu er svært rørig paa sin høie alder. ensjønt der har været mange tunge dage ogsaa før hende; hu var født i Wisconsin aa var me sin førældre en af di første som bosatte sig 14 *mil* sydwest fra Rochester. hendes mand døde aatte aar siden, saa hendes søn John *staapper* me hende. hu har sit hjem i Clearbrook nu. vi har nu været hær i 20 aar. aa liker nordre Minnesota gaat, de er fredeligt, me mange snille folk, baade i by aa paa *Farm*, aa megen Natursjønhed, saa vi trænger inte reise lange veie efter den. men vor bra de er, saa gaar vaare minder tilbake der vor vaar vugge stod. de synes ingen plas paa Jorden saa kjær. alt er saa levende aa hyggeligt. Tak før sist gode Venner aa slægtninger aa kom me non ord i posten, venlig hilsen til alle slegtninger aa Venner i N. Dakota aa i Minnesota. aa mange tak du Mrs L B før dit goe brev. Kom me flere slike, saa en venlig hilsen til bladets Personale aa læsere.

THE IMPACT OF ENGLISH ON AMERICAN-NORWEGIAN LETTER WRITING

REFERENCES

1. For further information about the language in these letters see the writer's forthcoming book, *The Norwegian Language in America: A Study in Bilingual Behavior*. Gratitude is hereby expressed to the staff of the newspaper for assistance and information.
2. Cf. Hans Bergersen, *Morsmålsoplæringen* 51-121 (Oslo, 1935).

On the Original of the Codex Regius of the Elder Edda

Didrik Arup Seip
University of Oslo

THE CODEX REGIUS of the Elder Edda (GkS 2365, 4to) is an Icelandic manuscript from about 1270. It is quite clear that large portions of it are a copy. In *Håndskrift Nr 2365, 4to gl. kgl. Samling* (Copenhagen, 1891) Wimmer and Jónsson state on page lxiii: "That our MS. is not original, but a copy of another or several other MSS., can be deduced with sufficient certainty from the mistakes it contains, many of which can only be explained on this assumption." In his introduction to *Corpus Codicum Islandicorum Medii Aevi*, X, Andreas Heusler has shewn that the greater part of GkS 2365, 4to must be a copy.

I do not intend to deal here with the question of the different kinds of precursors to the Codex Regius. Apart from what has been written in the two publications mentioned above, reference should be made to Finnur Jónsson's introduction to *De gamle Eddadigte* (Copenhagen, 1932) and Elias Wessen's introduction to "Fragments of the Elder and the Younger Edda" in *Corpus Cod. Isl. M. Aevi*," XVII.

I should, however, like to mention a number of features in the Codex Regius which it is reasonable to suppose derive from the original. This will give us an idea of the writing and language in the model or models.

First of all, I shall mention the peculiar use of *ð* for *d* after *l* and especially after *n*. In the introduction to *Norræn Fornkvæði* (1867) Bugge mentions twenty-one examples of *ð* for *d*. Of these there are two examples which seem to have been written with *d* + mark of abbreviation for the following syllable in the original: *arðaga, hroðreyrog*; there are three examples of *ld*: *giolð, helðr, halða;* and there are fifteen examples of *nd*: *onð, lanðit, fynðit, fronðr, lunði, Sigmunðr, granða, kinð, henði* (mistake for *henni*), *scunðoðo, rynenðr, henðr, stanða, grinðr, Funðo.* Now the Codex Regius frequently contains embellishments of the letter *d*, but it is not reasonable for such embellishments to have affected especially the combination *nd* and *ld*. The most reasonable explanation is that *ð* in this case has survived from the original. This practice was especially common in East Norwegian and the Tröndelag dialect, and is most probably an indication that the assimilation *nd, ld* had begun (cf. *Maal og minne*, 1945, pp. 15 ff. with references). These examples of *nd* and *ld* seem to point to the inevitable conclusion that there has been a written Norwegian original, direct or indirect, of the Codex Regius of the Elder Edda.

An obvious difference between Norwegian and Icelandic is to be seen in the use or non-use of *h* before *r, l, n*. In remoter days Norwegian had *h*, but in the eleventh century *h* disappears in Norwegian runic inscriptions (cf. Seip, *Norsk språkhistorie til omkring 1370*, pp. 62 ff.). In the case of Norwegian poetry from before the year 1000 we can expect to find *h* in these positions also in Norwegian. Thus in older poetry a preserved *h* is no indication whether it was originally Norwegian or Icelandic.

In the Hávamál 151 there is a line which runs: *rótom rás viðar*; *rás* is the genitive of *hrár* (adj.) and the alliteration shows that *h* has disappeared (cf. S. Bugge, *Norræn Fornkvæði*, p. 62; Egilsson-Jónsson, *Lexicon Poeticum*). The verse belongs to the Ljóðatal, which is generally considered to be Norwegian. The loss of *h* need not imply that the verse is more recent than the year 1050 in date, for the loss of *h* may of course have occurred in some Norwegian dialects at a comparatively early date. This example is no proof of a written Norwegian original of the

ON THE ORIGINAL OF THE CODEX REGIUS OF THE ELDER EDDA

Codex Regius. Other spellings, however, indicate that such was in fact the case. In Sigrdrífumál 15 we have *rungnis* for *hrungnis,* despite the fact that alliteration seems to demand *h*: *a þvi hveli er snys / undir reiþ Hrungnis* (cf. Bugge, *Norr. Fornkv.,* p. 231; Wimmer-Jónsson's edition, p. 161). It is for other reasons that the poem is regarded as Norwegian. The omission of *h*—in spite of alliteration—indicates a Norwegian written original.

The same may be said of a line in Helgakviða Hjǫrvarðssonar 20: *þott þu hafir hreina radd.* Here the *h* in *hreina* has been subsequently added, and *h* is in all probability incorrect. According to S. Bugge we should read *reina* from *reini* (masc.), i.e., stallion (S. Bugge, *Norr. Fornkv.,* p. 407). But the Icelandic scribe has mistaken the word and added *h* incorrectly. This shows that the scribe has had an original without *h* before *r*, i.e., a Norwegian written original. This poem, too, is usually regarded as Norwegian.

A number of other linguistic features in the Codex Regius point to a Norwegian original, and I shall briefly mention a few of them here:

Simplification of the diphthong in *siundo<sjaundu,* "the seventh," Grímn. 12, is probably Norwegian. The forms *siv* (7) and *siunda* are known from a number of old Icelandic manuscripts which usually appear to have Norwegian originals (cf. S. Bugge, *Norr. Fornkv.,* p. 307; Seip, ANF 64, p. 160).

In the Vǫluspá 19 *barmr* has been corrected to *baðmr.* The spelling with *r* in a word like this must have occurred in Norwegian (cf. Seip, *Norsk språkhistorie til omkring 1370,* pp. 121, 190; *Studier i norsk språkhistorie,* pp. 108-110).

For *landskjalftar* we have *landsciantar,* Lokasenna prosa (S. Bugge, *Norr. Fornkv.,* p. 123). This loss of *l* is characteristic of

[105]

Norwegian, but quite un-Icelandic (Seip, *Norsk språkhistorie til omkring 1370*, p. 114).

Another feature I should like to mention is that the combination *gn* is frequently written or corrected from *ngn*: frengna Hávamál 28; *igongn,* Reginsmál 59, and conversely *mangi* is written *magni,* Sigrdrifumál 12 (a hyper-Icelandicism). Likewise the metathesis *gils* for *gisl,* Lokasenna 34, points to a Norwegian original.

Finally I should mention that the original most probably used insular *n* similarly to *r.* Thus the scribe happens to write *retr* for *netr* (Helgakviða Hundingsbana 11 strophe 36).

There are other features we might cite, but what I have already mentioned proves conclusively that the Edda poems were written down in Norway, and that a Norwegian MS. was brought over to Iceland, probably before 1200.

Melkólfs saga ok Salomons Konungs[1]

Jess H. Jackson
The College of William and Mary

Í Þann tima er salamon son dauids ried fyrir jorsalalandi ok hann var kongr uordinn næst eftir david faudur sinn uitradi gud honum þat at hann mundi þa bæn ueita honum er hann bædi hann. En hann bad gud speki ok uitrleiks ok þat ueitti gud honum at hann uar uitrari en allir adrir menn i heiminum hafi uerid. Hann giordi þat mustari gudi til dyrdar er ekki hefir annat þuilikt verid i heiminum at uexti ok fegord þat var allt innan gulli buit ok af gulli gioruir allir hlutir þeir er þar voru til hafdir. hann hafdi ok med sier marga merkiliga menn ok uitra. Sa madr vox þar upp i iorsala borg er melkolfr het hann var bonda son einn. Þau fadir hans ok modir voru ecki mikils hattar ok ecki audig at peingvm þau unnu mikit syni sinum þat var kallat at eigi yxi sa madr vpp er vitrari væri at iofnum alldri en þessi sveinn ok ottuduz þau ef kongr yrdi varr vid uitrleik hans at hann mundi hann fra þeim taka. enn þau unnv honum svo mikit at þau mattu eigi af honum sia. ef þat var einn dag at þau fadir hans ok modir attu at uinna aa brott af gardinum þa lukti þau hann i lopti nockvru þui er þilid var umhuerfis ok eingu gluggr aa ok eigi rauf. hann var þa xii vetra gamall. Þann dag for salomon kongr aa maurk at skemta ser med hird sinni at beita i haukum sinum kongr var staddr einn saman vm daginn ok reid at husum þeim er fadir melkolfs [atti] þviat kongr hafdi spurt til uitrleika þessa sveins ok uill hann nu reyna hann ok er kongr kemr at husinu þui er þat lopt var ifir uppi er sueinninn var i þa stingr kongr augat annat or hesti er hann reid ok sva or haukinum ok ridr inn undir husid ok spyrr huart þar se nockur madr. Er her madr sagdi melkolfr kongr spyrr huersu morg eru her

[107]

augu. ui segir sueinninn. hui vi segir kongr. sueinninn segir þu hefir ii auga hestr þinn eit auga ok haukr þinn hefir i auga ok ek hefi ii auga. Þu ert uitr suein segir kongr ok uil ek at þu farir heim med mer. sueinninn segir þessa bods kann ek þauck en eigi ma ek þo fyrst at sinni med ydr fara. hui sætir þæt segir kongr þviat fadir minn ok modir min vnna mer sua mikit at þau munu ganga af vitinv ef ek er horfinn ok mvnv þau ætla at mer se tortimt er þau sia her blod. En ver munum koma til yduar oll saman litlu sidar ok sua giordv þau at þau koma til kongs ok fengv godar uidrtaukur. En melkolfr uar med kongi ok mikils virdr ok var hinn mesti spekingr. Eitt huert sinn þa er kongr for heiman þa setti hann melkolf til at styra hirdinne ok dæma oll mal en þat er sagt at ii hirdmenn aufund [ud] uz var annar audigr ok slæguitr ok undir hyggiu fullr en annar var oslægr ok godgiarnari ok vinsælli ok hafdi sa meiri uirding af kongi. En hinn aufundar þat ok uilldi fyrir koma honum. einn aptan satu þeir vid dryckiu ok drack sa fast hinn vuitrari ok feck aa hann miok ok uissi hann fatt huat hann mællti. Þa mællti hinn uitrari þat uillda ek at uel væri med ockr ok idrunz ek er ek hefi eigi uerit uel til þin. Giarna uillda ek at uel væri sagdi hinn vuitrari madr. ok þat til marks ef þu uill selia mier slatr vist nockura þa uil ek kaupa at þer en ek man giallda þer fyrer sidar. Þat vil ek uist sagdi [hinn] audgari en huersu mikit slatr uilltu hafa litid sagdi hinn oaudgari ek hefir af þer sidu en þu hefir af mer adra sidar ok nu iatter hinn þessu ok færir honum slatr uistina. Stundu sidar heimtir hinn audgari ok hann sagdis uist skylldu fa honom naut sidu ek uil uist sagdi hinn hafa af þer sidu sem mælt var med ockr. Þa finnr hinn*****[2]

Translation[3]

In the time when Solomon son of David ruled over Jerusalem and had become king, next after David his father, God revealed to him that He would grant him any boon which he should ask Him. And he asked God for wisdom and sagacity; and God granted him that he was wiser than all other men in the world have been. To the honor of God he built that temple like which there has not been another in the world in size and beauty. Within, it was all adorned with gold, and of gold were made all things that were for use there.

He [Solomon] had also with him many remarkable men and wise. That man grew up there in Jerusalem who was named Melkolf. He was a farmer's son. His father and mother were not of importance and not rich. They loved their son much. It was said that the man did not grow up who, at the same age, was wiser than this boy; and they feared that, if the King became aware of his wisdom, he would take him [away] from them. And they loved him so much that they could not do without him. If there was a day when his father and mother had to work away from home, they locked him in a loft that was boarded [up] all round, with no window and no hole. He was then twelve years old.

One day King Solomon went to the forest with his men to amuse himself by hunting with his hawks. The King was stationed quite alone during the day, and he rode to the house that Melkolf's father [had], because he had heard about the wisdom of this boy, and he wants to try him. And when the king came to the house with the loft up over it and the boy inside, he stabs out one eye of the horse that he rode and also [one] out of the hawk, and rides in and under the house, and asks whether there was anybody there.

"Yes, there is somebody here," said Melkolf.

The King asks how many eyes there are here.

"Six," says the boy.

"Wherefore six?" says the King.

The boy says, "You have two eyes, your horse one eye and your hawk has one eye, and I have two eyes."

"You are a keen boy," says the King, "and I want you to go home with me."

The boy says, "I am grateful for this offer, although I cannot at the present go with you."

"What is the reason for that?" says the King.

"Because my father and my mother love me so much that they will go out of their wits if I have disappeared, and they will suppose that I have been killed upon seeing blood here. But we will come to you all together a little later."

And they came to the King and were well received. And Melkolf was with the King and thought much of and was the greatest sage.

One time when the King went away from home, he set Melkolf to steer the men and to give judgment in all suits. And it is said that two of the men bore grudges against each other. One of them was rich and cunnning and false, and the other was frank and more kindly and blessed with friends, and had the greater honor from the King. But the other one envies that and wished to destroy him.

One evening they sat drinking, and the less wise one drank deep and got very tight and little knew what he said. Then said the wiser one, "I wish that all were well between us, and I repent that I have not been friendly with you."

"Yes; I wish all were well," said the less wise one.

"—And let this be for a token: if you will sell me some butcher's meat, I will buy [it] from you and pay you for [it] later."

"Surely, I will do that," said the rich one, "but how much meat do you want?"

"[Just a] little," said the poorer one. "I will take a side from you, and you shall have a side of me later."

And now agrees the other one to this, and he delivers to him the butcher's meat. A little later, he demands his debt, and the debtor said he would get him a side of meat.

"I will certainly," said the creditor, "have a side of you as was fixed between us."

Then finds the [other]*****

Two groups of documents with similar titles are liable to confusion with *Melkólfs saga ok Salomons konungs*.[4] One group is represented in English by the Old English poem *Solomon and Saturn* and the prose *Dialogues of Solomon and Saturn*.[5] The poem "like the Norse *Wafþrudnismal* [Vafþrúðnismál] ... is at times a gnomic type of dialogue."[6] A characteristic of the group is gnomic or riddling detail. The Scandinavian manuscripts, all paper and late, label the dialogue either *samtale* or *saga*. The other group contains a widespread oriental story of magic and taboo called Salomon and Morolf, or some variant.[7] Like the preceding group, this one has little to do with the *Markólfs saga ok Salomons konungs*. Yet some details of all three overlap.

Certain details of the fragment suggest three well-known folk motifs: 1) propounding riddles to test cleverness, 2) the grateful dead man, and 3) the bond or the pound of flesh.

Since the Queen of Sheba went to Jerusalem to propound riddles to Solomon,[8] this technique for testing cleverness has been practiced. The riddle of the sphinx is a capital example; the story of Antiochus and his daughter in *Pericles, Prince of Tyre* is another. Instances and variants are legion. From the hundreds listed in Stith Thompson's *Motif-Index* (III, 325-356), two approximate the two in the fragment (H583.1 and H583.1.1).

The King is questioning a clever youth, who answers in riddles: King asks (H583.1), "What do you see?" Boy answers, "One and a half men and a horse's head." (Himself, the legs of the King on horseback in the door, and the horse's head.) King

(H583.1.1): "Are you alone at home?" Boy: "Not now; I see the half of two quadrupeds." (Two legs of the King and the forefeet of his horse.)

The boy Melkolf in the fragment has to be keen-eyed and observant to answer Solomon's query; there is no door for him to see through and, being locked in a boarded-up loft without window or hole, he obviously has to peep through the floor to see that the King, who has ridden up *under* the house, has put out one of his horse's eyes and one of his hawk's, and to answer accurately that the King, he, the horse, and the hawk together have two eyes short of the normal number. Or maybe he was familiar with the question already. Even so, at twelve he was clever.

Melkolf's answer to the King's question as to whether there was anybody at home hardly demonstrates mental superiority; it appears to be merely a traditional question natural in beginning a riddling series.

Obviously, the fragment presents a variant of riddles propounded to test cleverness, as later details indicate: Melkolf became one of the King's prized men, the King adjudged him keen, he was recognized as one of the wisest men of his time, and the King left him to rule in his stead when he went away from home.

Whether the other folk motif is a variant of the grateful dead man or of the pound of flesh (if it is either) is harder to decide. To be brief, I will try to derive the formulae of these two motives and then select such examples as seem most pertinent to the inquiry.

The nucleus of the thankful dead man formula (the simple theme) should run somewhat like this: a man provides burial for a corpse. The grateful spirit of the corpse helps the man to fortune on condition that he get half the gains. Later, the spirit claims half of all (e.g., money, land, wife, and child).

Professor Gerould's version, in the records of the English Folk-Lore Society, is this: "A man finds a corpse lying unburied, and out of pure philanthropy procures interment for it at great personal inconvenience. Later he is met by the ghost of the dead man, who in many cases promises him help on the condition of receiving, in return, half of what he gets. The hero obtains a wife (or some other reward), and, when called upon, is ready to fulfil his bargain as to sharing his possessions."[9]

Since the metrical romance *Sir Amadace* is, as Professor Kittredge said, "the last development of the grateful dead man" and somewhat similar in at least one detail to the fragment, I abridge Wells's summary of it:[10] Sir Amadace, a spendthrift knight, mortgages all and departs with forty pounds and a few attendants. He finds a woman grieving beside the dead body of her lord, denied burial by a creditor. He provides burial. On his way, he is met by a knight in white who directs him to wrecked ships with supplies adequate for making suit to a king's daughter; it is stipulated that he will give the knight half of all he gains. He marries the princess and fathers a son. The white knight turns up, demands not only half of the money and of the kingdom, but literally half of the wife and half of the son. As the knight is about to cut the wife in two first (she being the dearer), the white knight stops him, divulging that he is the grateful spirit of the dead man. He commends Sir Amadace's generosity, and his wife's honor in fulfilling pledges.[11]

This is the simple theme of a widespread story, the oldest version of which is found in the story of Tobit in the Apocrypha, where it occurs in combination and in variation: it includes the theme of the poison maiden (Sara, the woman possessed by the demon Asmodeus, who, on the wedding night, killed each of her seven husbands); and in it the grateful dead man has been supplanted by the angel Rafael.

One or two examples of the tale with the simple theme assembled by Professor Gerould[12] are promising in that they suggest the rawness of the fragment.

In one, a Greek youth was helped in love by an old man (substituting for the grateful dead man) who exacted a promise of half of what he got. On the wedding night, the old man knocked on the door of the bridal chamber and demanded that the bride be divided. As the groom prepared to cut her in two, the intruder said that he wanted only to test his fidelity.[13]

Another (*Rittertriuwe*, p. 36) contains the spendthrift knight, the ransoming and burial of a dead man, and the ghost of the corpse as a stranger knight demanding half of all gains. On the second night after the wedding, the stranger entered the bridal room and claimed a share in the marital rites.

Several others grant an option between the lady and the whole kingdom or other possessions.[14]

Thompson lists others[15] but none closer to that of the fragment.

None of these seem very close. Yet one must remember that only one detail of this formula (if it be this formula) is found in the fragment. Could one maintain that Portia of Belmont or Rappacini's daughter are not perilous princesses (or poison maidens or dangerous women) because the full formula of the woman who for some reason or other is dangerous to men is not present? or that the riddling and the dangerous woman in *Pericles* and the sphinx at the gate of Thebes, as well as *The Taming of the Shrew*, do not all involve the same story or formula? Can one identify the detail in this fragment of Solomon and Melkolf with this type? One cannot be sure.

Shakespeare's bond story in *The Merchant of Venice* is typical of the *Fleischpfand* kind of narrative. Stripped of entanglements and superfluities, the formula is this: A Christian merchant borrows money from a Jew for the use of a friend. The lender takes a bond granting a pound of flesh in forfeit. In court, the lender demands a literal interpretation. A stranger judge foils him by literal pleading: an exact pound is to be cut, and no blood must be shed.

The Variorum *Merchant of Venice* cites various analogues and examples.

1) In *Gesta Romanorum* (MS. Harl. 7333, *ca.* 1400): for penalty, "to draw away alle flesh of thi body froo the bone, with a sharp swerde"; lady in disguise as a lawyer; double money offered in lieu of the flesh (as in *The Merchant of Venice*); no shedding of blood.

2) One still older is from the *Mahabharata* (*ca.* 300 B. C.): A falcon demands a pigeon from a king who is protecting it. The king offers various substitutes, and finally an equal weight of his own flesh. Scales are brought (as in *The Merchant of Venice*); the pigeon is placed in one pan. The king cuts a piece of his flesh that seems large enough but proves too light. He cuts again and again; then he gets bodily into the scale-pan.

3) *The Orator* (of "Alexander Siluayn"—pseudonym for van den Busche. London, 1576): No more than just a pound to be cut.

4) A Hindu legend says that a dove (pigeon? which would weigh about a pound) took refuge from a hawk in the god's breast. The hawk tore from the god's breast flesh weighing as much as the dove; but blood fell to the ground and wrote the scriptures of the Vedas.

5) The oldest reference to the story in English is from the *Cursor Mundi* (end of 13th century): A Christian goldsmith was, upon default, to pay in flesh the weight of the money that he owed to a Jew, who would take eyes, hands, tongue, nose, and so on. No blood was to be shed.

6) The ballad of *Gernutus* (from *Percy's Reliques,* 1765, 1,

191): The flesh is to come from under the right side; the Jew whets his knife (as some Shylocks do); the bond is a "merrie jest" (as in *The Merchant of Venice*).

7) In a French version (Corrozet's *Divers propos mémorables*, 1577, p. 77): Instead of a pound of flesh, "one of the party's eyes shall be pulled out."

8) "By the severe Roman law of The Twelve Tables, creditors could cut to pieces their debtors upon proof of their debt, and without any express provision when the loan was made, and they need be under no restriction as to the exact amount of their slice." (Pp. 308-309.)

9) In an Italian story, a Jew is determined to cut the pound of flesh from the debtor's privates. (P. 295.)

10) A Latin version written in England but set in Denmark (p. 314): Two brothers seal a *Fleischpfand* bargain; no substitution is to be acceptable, no drop of blood is to be shed, and there is complete lack of fraternal sympathy.

The similarity between the Solomon and Melkolf episode and these versions lies, I think, in the motive behind the bond, in the savageness of the details, and in the literal pleading represented in the fragment by the sentence: "ek hefir af ther sidu en thu hefir af mer adra sidar" ("I will take a side from you, and you shall have a side of me later"). More than a pound of flesh is involved, whether it come from a beef or the debtor; but the *Fleischpfand* does not restrict itself to just sixteen ounces, as the evidence shows. Furthermore, in the fragment and in some of the other versions, the purpose of the creditor is murder.

The evidence at hand is inconclusive. The character of the bargain in the fragment (one recalls the inutility of paying the forfeit in human flesh—unless perhaps "to bait fish withal"—the merry jest as a motive, the literal pleading, and the double meaning) resembles the pound of flesh story. *Per contra*, the amplitude of the operation (a whole side of a human carcass comparable in size to a side of slaughtered butcher's meat) hints at the gory division of wife and son found in the story of the grateful dead man. In general, the flavor of the fragment is oriental: the Hebrew connections "gehen in ihren Grundlagen auf hebräische Tradition zurück";[16] the riddling of the famous queen on her visit to Solomon is obvious; the *Fleischpfand* and the grateful dead man both have definite representatives in Eastern folk tradition. One hypothesis is that the piece is Byzantine. Exchange either way between East and West seems possible.[17]

REFERENCES

1. The unique parchment manuscript of this fragment, AM. 696, 4to, preserved in the Library of the University of Copenhagen, contains 33 pieces called various fragments, from the 13-16th centuries. No. III, consisting of two leaves about 20x14 cm., from *ca.* 1400, contains (on leaf 1) *Melkólfs* (usually written "Markólfs") *saga ok Salomons konungs*; and (on leaf 2) *Placidus saga*, a fragment covering pp. 209-210 of *Heilagra manna sögur*, vol. 2 (ed. by C. R. Unger, Christiania, 1877). Both are in the same hand. Since the two leaves were once used for binding some small quarto volume, 1-recto and 2-verso are badly rubbed.

For the opportunity to make this transcription, I am obligated to the American Council of Learned Societies, whose favors to me while I was one of their Fellows were —and have since been—both liberal and numerous.

I also record my thanks to Professor C. N. Gould, who first called this manuscript to my notice, and to Professor Jón Helgason for help in transcribing.

2. The semi-diplomatic transcription I have used before, in *Sigurðar saga fóts ok Ásmundar Húnakongs*. See *PMLA*, XLVI (December, 1931), 999, and note 112.

3. I supply a translation for convenience, in the hope that I may get suggestions for identifying the fragment.

4. Finnur Jónsson says (*Den oldnorske og oldislandske Litteraturs Historie*, I-III, anden udgave [Köbenhavn, 1920], III, 112): "Den saga, den herved menes, er saa vidt vides, fuldstændig tabt, undtagen for saa vidt som der i AM 696 III findes et blad deraf; i fölge dette er Markolf en hövding og en af Salomons mænd. Hvad der ellers findes under titlen "Samtal Markolfs og Salomons" (i mange hdskrr.) har intet med denne saga at göre; det er gengivelse af en fremmed original og bestaar kun af samtaler, hvor Markolf, der er den hæsligste og laveste skabning, overbyder sig selv med grove, plumpheder. Det produkt vedkommer os ikke."

5. Ed. by J. M. Kemble, *The Dialogues of Solomon and Saturn*, London, 1848. Two manuscripts from Corpus Christi College, Cambridge, nos. 41 and 422, contain both the poem and the prose dialogues.

6. George K. Anderson, *The Literature of the Anglo-Saxons* (Princeton, 1949), p. 184.

7. See *Die deutschen Dichtungen von Salmon und Morolf*, l. Band, hrsg. von Friedrich Vogt (Halle, 1880). 2. Band, *Salomon und Markolf*, hrsg. von Walter Hartmann

(Halle, 1934); *Salomon et Marcolfus*, hrsg. von Walter Benary (Sammlateinischer Texte, hrsg. von Alfons Hilka, Bd.8) (Heidelberg, 1913); and W. Schaumberg, "Sprüchgedicht Salomo und Morolf," *PBB* 2 (1896), 1-63.

8. See 1 *Kings*, 10 and 2 *Chronicles*, 9.

"Der Ursprung der Salomo-Dialoge liegt letzten Endes in den Salomo zugeschriebenen Büchern des alten Testamentes, denn seine Weisheit ist hier eben in Sprüchen niedergelegt. Die dialogische Form dieser Didaktik wird erwähnt bei dem Besuch der Königin von Saba, denn sie kam ihn zu versüchen in Rätseln."—G. Ehrismann, *Geschichte der deutschen Literatur bis zum Ausgang des Mittelalters* (München, 1922), II (part 1), 326.

9. G. H. Gerould, *The Grateful Dead*, Publications of the Folk-Lore Society, LX, London, 1907, p. x.

10. John Edwin Wells, *A Manual of the Writings in Middle English*, 1050-1400 (New Haven, 1926), pp. 159-160.

11. The romance was edited for the Camden Society by John Robson, *Three Early English Metrical Romances*, London, 1842, pp. 27-56.

12. Gerould, *op. cit.*, pp. 26-43.

13. *Ibid.*, pp. 29-30.

14. *Ibid.*, *Lion de Bourges*, p. 34, *Dianese*, p. 35, and *Old Swedish*, pp. 25-36.

15. E341 and E341.1 in *Motif-Index*, II, 364-365.

16. Ehrismann, *op. cit.*, II (part 1), 315.

17. This study is a revised version of a paper read by invitation at the fortieth annual meeting of the Society for the Advancement of Scandinavian Study at St. Olaf College, Northfield, Minnesota, in May, 1950.

Wilhelm Grimm's Letters to Peter Erasmus Müller

P. M. MITCHELL

University of Kansas

THE PUBLICATION IN 1885 of the *Briefwechsel der Gebrüder Grimm mit nordischen Gelehrten* by Ernst Schmidt made an illuminating contribution to the history of Scandinavian-German literary relations and revealed the debt of the Grimms to several Scandinavian scholars, foremost among them Rasmus Nyerup and Rasmus Rask. Numerous details of this correspondence remained undivulged because many letters were missing; in particular there was a paucity of extant letters from the Grimms themselves. In his introduction Ernst Schmidt complained that no letters from the Grimms to Børge Thorlacius, Peter Erasmus Müller, Finnur Magnússon, or Christian Molbech had been preserved. The queries and opinions which the letters of the Grimms had contained could, it seemed, only be deduced from the replies of these Danish scholars.

Fortunately, some of Wilhelm Grimm's letters to two of the above-mentioned scholars, Peter Erasmus Müller and Finnur Magnússon, do exist. In 1922 a short letter by Wilhelm Grimm to P. E. Müller, postmarked 6 July 1817, was published in the *Anzeiger für deutsches Altertum*, IV, 202-204. Where and how the letter had been preserved, as well as the whereabouts of the letter, were not mentioned. This letter was written in answer to P. E. Müller's letter of 13 April [?] 1817 (reproduced in *Briefwechsel*, pp. 140-142). It contains an expression of thanks for the diplomas of the Scandinavian Literary Society which had been sent to Wilhelm and Jacob Grimm, brief remarks about P. E. Müller's *Sagabibliothek* and divers other works pertaining to medieval Germany and Scandinavia. This letter is but one of six to P. E. Müller which are extant.

Among the many letters to the Danish theologian and antiquarian Peter Erasmus Müller (1776-1834) preserved in the Royal Library in Copenhagen are five letters by Wilhelm Grimm. Two letters by Wilhelm Grimm to the Icelandic scholar Finnur Magnússon are preserved in the Danish National Archives in Copenhagen. The letters to P. E. Müller are reproduced here. I hope to be able to prepare the letters to Finnur Magnússon for publication by 1952.

Wilhelm Grimm's letters to P. E. Müller are nos. 148-152 in Ny Kgl. Samling 3747-4°, in the Royal Library. The oldest of the letters is in poor condition; there are several lacunae caused by the edge of the paper's having been broken or torn off. There are only a few lacunae in the later letters. As a whole, the letters are written in German script and in a fairly clear hand, although several words have been difficult to decipher.

For Wilhelm Grimm, P. E. Müller was above all the editor of the *Sagabibliothek med Anmærkninger og indledende Afhandlinger* I-III, Copenhagen, 1817-1820, the first attempt to present collectively Old Norse-Icelandic saga literature in translation. Even today, it is still a valuable reference work. The Grimm-Müller correspondence nevertheless antedates the publication of the *Sagabibliothek*; it had its origins in a common interest in the Danish folksong, i.e., the "*kæmpevise*." A critique of the new edition of the Danish folksongs by Abrahamson, Nyerup, and Rahbek is the substance of Wilhelm Grimm's first letter to P. E. Müller.

By 1816, P. E. Müller was known in Germany through two of his works which had been translated in German. The first was *Ueber die Aechtheit der Asalehre und den Werth der Snorroischen Edda.... Aus der Handschrift übersetzt von L. C. Sander,*

WILHELM GRIMM'S LETTERS TO PETER ERASMUS MÜLLER

Professor, Copenhagen, 1811, a repudiation of the attempts by A. L. Schlözer, J. C. Adelung, and Friedrich Rühs to invalidate Old Norse-Icelandic literature as historical evidence. The second was *Ueber den Ursprung und Verfall der isländischen Historiographie, nebst einem Anhange über die Nationalität der altnordischen Gedichte . . . übersetzt von L. C. Sander,* Copenhagen, 1813, in which P. E. Müller championed Old Norse-Icelandic literature against the charges made by Friedrich Rühs in *Die Edda. Nebst einer Einleitung über nordische Poesie und Mythologie und einem Anhang über die historische Literatur der Isländer,* Berlin, 1812. Wilhelm Grimm had reviewed P. E. Müller's *Ueber die Aechtheit der Asalehre* in *Heidelbergische Jahrbücher der Literatur,* Jahrgang IV, Band II, pp. 774 f., and had himself attacked Rühs' book in *Heidelbergische Jahrbücher,* Jahrgang V, 1812, Nr. 61-62 and again in a rebuttal in Jahrgang VI, 1813, *Intelligenzblatt* II, pp. 10-13.

Taken together, Wilhelm Grimm's letters to P. E. Müller reflect, first, the attitude of the Grimms and the majority of German scholars toward Old Norse-Icelandic literature and their penchant for the idea of a *gemeingermanische Literatur*; second, the dependence of German upon Danish scholarship as far as the Old Scandinavian literature is concerned, during the first three decades of the century; and, third, the contest between the Grimms and Friedrich Heinrich von der Hagen (who is not mentioned here by name) to be the first to publish the lays of the so-called Elder Edda in Germany.

The earliest letter is undated, but must have been written late in 1815 or early in 1816. Wilhelm Grimm refers to the preface of his *Altdänische Heldenlieder,* published in 1811, as having been written five years before. The Grimms' partial edition of the Elder Edda, a copy of which Wilhelm Grimm mentions sending to P. E. Müller at the same time as the letter, appeared in 1815.

The edition of an old German poem "ietzt erst fertig geworden" refers to the Grimms' edition of Hartmann von der Aue's *Der arme Heinrich*, which bears the imprint Berlin 1815. The penciled date, 1813, on the holograph in the Royal Library is therefore incorrect. This letter is significant if only because of Wilhelm Grimm's admission that he previously had misinterpreted the relation of skaldic to popular poetry. Rühs' hypothesis, referred to by Wilhelm Grimm, was that "Die ganze alte norwegische Geschichte von den Zeiten Harald Schönhaars ist völlig *grundlose* Erdichtung" (Rühs, *op. cit.*, 1812, p. 277) and that Old Norse-Icelandic literature comprised only borrowings from foreign sources, first and foremost Anglo-Saxon.

1.

Prof. Müller zu Copenhagen

Hochwürdiger,
Hochgeehrtester Herr!

Hr. Prof. Wolke[1] hat mir Ew. Hochw. Preisschrift über die Wichtigkeit der isländ. Sprache[2] vor einiger Zeit als er von Berlin zurückkehrte, selbst überbracht. Ich danke Ihnen für dies schöne Geschenk recht sehr, das ich mit grossem Vergnügen gelesen; es scheint mir seinen Gegenstand mit ebenso viel gründlicher Gelehrsamkeit als Klarheit und Eindringlichkeit zu erörtern. Dasselbe gilt von Ihrer Schrift über die isländ. Geschichtschr[eibung][3] worin mir besonders die gesammelten Züge des haüslichen und [des] öffentlichen Lebens lieb waren; ein solches Werk, soweit es [von] sämmtlichen noch erhaltenen Quellen gestatten, ins Grosse [...] ausgeführt müsste von entschiedenem Erfolge seyn. Was ich über[all] in Ihren Schriften schätze, ist die Freiheit des Umblicks, das eigenth[ümliche] Gefühl für das lebendige und das Streben, die Kenntniss des alten als eingreifend und wirksam für uns darzustellen. Würdig[t] auch ein jeder wie Sie, bei der durchaus natürlichen und lobe[ns]würdigen Anhänglichkeit und Liebe für das einheimische, auc[h...] Streben und Verdienst, so würde von keiner Seite eine Klage entstehen können. Die Hypothese des Rühs haben Sie gar wohl widerlegt und wäre der Gegner ein anderer und eine Bekehrung möglich, so müsste er sich wohl besinnen, allein, was er an Vernunft hat, das geht ihn sogleich verloren, wenn er Widerspruch hört und es ist auf keine Weise bei ihm etwas zu gewinnen.

Auch die mir von Nyerup zugeschickte Recension Ew. Hochw. über die neue Ausgabe der Kämpe wiser[4] (ich wünsche der alte, gleichsam volksthümliche Name, mag er immerhin nicht umfassend seyn, wäre beibehalten) habe ich mit Theilnahme gelesen. Was Sie an dem Buche selbst tadeln, das Auslassen einiger guten u. merkwürdigen Stücke habe ich auch daran auszusetzen gehabt, sonst verdient es viel Lob und ich wünschte, dass wir Deutsche eine ebensosorgfältige Ausgabe unserer Volkslieder hätten. Nur in einer Rücksicht habe ich mich in meiner Erwartung getäuscht gesehen, indem ich gehofft, das Sammeln der noch ietzt unter dem dänischen Volk lebendigen Gesanges würde eine reichlichere Ernte gewährt haben, da nur einzelne Lieder daher gekommen sind. Bei uns würde diese Quelle oben an stehen und aus ihr sind die schönsten Lieder im Wunderhorn geflossen. Ich kann nicht glauben, dass schon Wedel, Syv[5] und die übrigen benutzten Handschriften schon alles aufgefasst haben, und es mag in der Lage der Herausgeber liegen, da es von der Stadt aus allerdings schwer hält, zu so etwas zu gelangen.

Für das, was Ew. Hochw. über meine Ansichten in der Vorrede der [a]llerdings mancher Verbesserung fähigen Übersetzung der Kämpe-Viser[6] bemerkt haben, danke ich Ihnen. Es ist aus keinem andern Grunde gekommen als der Sache selbst zu nützen und die Wahrheit zu fördern und dahin geht ja alle unsere Arbeit. Seitdem ich jenes geschrieben sind fünf Jahre verflossen und da habe ich manche Lücke in meinen Kenntnissen ausfüllen und manche Ansicht berichtigen können. Dass ich den Gegensatz zwischen Skalden und Volksdichtung falsch aufgestellt, darin haben Sie vollkommen Recht, es lag daran, dass ich damals die eddischen Lieder von den Wolsungen nur aus Bruchstücken kennen konnte. Jetzt nachdem ich sie gelesen und über ihr Wesen nachgedacht habe, bin ich zwar überzeugt, dass sie in ihrer Einfachheit und Grösse zwar Lieder waren, die das ganze Volk mit Lust hörte und verstehen konnte, aber sie sind doch nicht Volkslieder in dem Sinn, in welchem es die Kämpe-Viser sind und verhalten sich zu diesen etwa wie das Nibelungenlied, als Ganzes, zu den einzelnen, kleinen, epischen. Insofern die Zeiten der Abfassung so sehr verschieden sind stehen die eddischen und die Kämpe-Viser in einem sehr bestimmten Gegensatz. Dagegen verhalten sich die spätern, die künstlichen und überkünstlichen Skaldenlieder zu den K. V. wie Kunstdichtung zur Volksdichtung; wenn ich gesagt, die Skalden hätten einen besondern Stand gebildet, so meine ich darunter nicht, dass sie sich politisch abgesondert, aber das Geschäft selbst gab ihrem Leben doch unbezweifelt einen eigenthümlichen Ausdruck und ein eigenthümliches Verhältnis zum übrigen. Ähnlich haben sich die Meistersänger aus den freiern und edlern Verhaltnissen [sic] der Minnesänger in engere Schranken zurückgezogen.

Wenn Sie die Lieder der Kämpe-V. welche die alte uns Germanen gemeinschaftliche Sage darstellen für eine Mischung altdeutscher und altdänischer Dichtkunst halten, so sind wir nicht weit von einander entfernt, denn ich habe S. 430 etwas ähnliches ausgedruckt. Dagegen scheint mir noch immer, was Sie geneigt sind für unmittelbare Übersetzung aus dem Deutschen zu halten, also für die Arbeit Einzelner, vielmehr aus einer lebendigen Vereinigung entstanden. Es finden sich Züge, die unzweifelhaft mit der nordischen Sage und blos mit ihr übereinstimmen: glauben Sie, dass diese aus den alten Liedern von Kennern derselben entlehnt sind? Ich getraue nicht beizustimmen, denn es streitet gegen das Wesen der Volkslieder und sie würden in diesem Falle keine ächten geworden seyn; auch ist der ähnliche Fall in dem Lied von dem gestohlenen Hammer dagegen, welches auch aus lebendiger Überlieferung nicht aus einer Bearbeitung des alten Lieds entstanden ist. Haben sich jene Züge aber im Leben erhalten und durch Ueberlieferung fort gepflanzt, so kann ich mir auch nicht denken, dass die mit der deutschen Sage übereinkommende Elemente aus Büchern oder sonst einer nicht dem Volk zugehörigen Quelle könnten geflossen seyn. Gar, wie sollte die nach der deutschen Sage erzählte Rache der Chrimhild auf der Insel Hven ihre so bedeutende Örtlichkeit gewonnen haben, wenn sie erst durch eine deutsche Übersetzung bekannt geworden wäre.

Ich glaube, dass noch manches sich aufklären würde, wenn man auch die sogenannten prosaischen Volkssagen dort sammelte, namentlich auf den kleinen Inseln wo sich manches hinflüchtet und rettet, das in der grössern Bewegung des von der Hauptstadt abhangenden Landes untergeht. Sollte niemand dazu geneigt seyn? die Prediger, die sich so thätig und geschickt bei Ihren trefflichen National-Museum selbst bei der Sammlung der Melodien[7] gezeigt, könnten vieles thun, es kommt nur darauf an, dass sie von dem Werth der Sache überzeugt werden. Wir haben in dieser Absicht die unter dem Volk lebenden Märchen gesammelt und es hat sich mancher überraschende Aufschluss ergeben. Doch ich will meinem Brief eine Gränze setzen.

Beikommend bin ich so frei, zugleich im Namen meines Bruders, Ihnen den ersten Theil unserer Edda[8] zu senden, betrachten Sie ihn mit Güte und Nachsicht; so wie auch die Ausgabe eines an sich gewiss schönen altdeutschen Gedichts,[9] die ietzt erst fertig geworden ist. Uber diese Schriften Ihr Urtheil zu vernehmen, wird uns sehr lieb seyn. Wir beide empfehlen uns Ihnen mit der aufrichtigsten Hochachtung.

Ew. Hochwürden
ergebenster
W. C. Grimm.

Grimm's letter of November 22, 1816, is a reply to P. E. Müller's letter of November 5 of the same year. Müller had written explaining the arrangements which had been made with Carl Lachmann and the Reimersche Buchhandlung about the translation and publication of the first volume of Müller's *Sagabibliothek*. P. E. Müller's manuscript had been returned to him without explanation and he erroneously concluded that his work had been neither translated nor printed. The entire misunderstanding as well as the reason for various errors in the German translation of the *Sagabibliothek* are explained by Lachmann in a letter to P. E. Müller dated June 4, 1826, and now preserved in the Royal Library in Copenhagen, Ny Kgl. Samling 3747-4°. Müller enquired whether the Grimms would consider translating the work.

2.

Cassel 27de Nov. 1816.

Wohlgeborner,
Hochgeehrtester Herr Professor.

Je wichtiger mir bei grosser Neigung für die nordische Literatur eine Sagenbibliothek und von Ihnen ausgearbeitet seyn musste, desto unangenehmer war mir die Nachricht von der Stockung des Werks, welche Ihr werther Brief vom 5.^{t} D. M. enthielt. Sie kam mir ganz unerwartet, da mir von Berlin aus längst das Buch als eine gewisse Erscheinung angekündigt war, auch das Betragen des Hn. Reimers,[10] des Besitzers der Realschulbuchhandlung, konnte ich nicht erklären. Nun wäre ich aus Liebe zur Sache und aus einer aufrichtigen Hochachtung Ihrer gelehrten Arbeiten wohl geneigt gewesen, den Vorschlag anzunehmen, obgleich wir beide in dieser Zeit mannichfach beschäftigt sind und die Übersetzung daher schwerlich in der kürzesten Frist hätte fertig werden können; Indess eh ich Ihnen antwortete und bei [...] Buchhandlungen anfragte, wollte ich erst in [...] Erkundigungen einziehen, wie die Sache sich verhalten und was Ursache dieses seltsamen Abbrechens gewesen, zumal ich mit Hn Reimer in freundschaftlichen Verhältnissen stehe und ihm immer als einen liberalen und geraden Mann gefunden. So eben erhalte ich nun die Antwort, dass das Werk bereits fertig gedruckt ist und in diesem Augenblick schon versendet wird. Wahrscheinlich ist Ihre Handschrift, nach Beendigung des Gebrauchs zurückgeschickt worden und zwar ohne weitern Nachricht dabei, weil das Buch selbst bald folgen sollte.

Ich freue mich über diese angenehme Entwickelung und eile Sie davon zu benachrichtigen, da mein Brief doch wohl eher anlangt, als das Buch auf der fahrenden Post und ein Brief des Hn Lachmann von Königsberg einen längern Weg hat. Ich lege das mir zugeschickte Titelblatt bei.

Zwar ist hier durch die Gelegenheit einer nähern Verbindung mit Ew. Wohlgeb. verschwunden, indessen [...]te ich doch auf die Fortdauer Ihrer freundschaftlichen [Gesin]nung und in Vertrauen darauf, komme ich auch mit einer angelegentlichen Bitte. Der zweite Band der von meinem Bruder und mir herausgegebenen Edda bleibt noch zurück, weil wir doch das jenige was die neue grosse Ausgabe des Instituts,[11] auf die wir schon so lange gewartet, ohne Zweifel gewähren wird, gern benutzen wollen. Wir geben bekanntlich *blos* die Lieder, die in den Fabelkreis der Nibelungen fallen und die Erklärung derselben, welche einen besondern Band ausmacht, ist mit die Hauptarbeit unseres Unternehmens, das gewiss auch in vielen andern [Hin] sichten der dortigen Ausgabe nachstehen wird. Wollten Sie, wenn es Ihnen ohne Mühe möglich ist un[s die] bisher schon gedruckten, aber nicht ausgegebenen B[ogen] des Buchs ietzt schon mittheilen? Besonders käme es uns a[uf] Gunnars slagr an, wovon wir den vollständigen Te [xt] noch nicht besitzen. Ich darf voraussetzen, dass [Sie] uns keinen Missbrauch zutrauen werden; was w[ir] von dorther erhalten, soll treulich angemerkt werden. Ich brauche nicht zu sagen, welch einen grossen Gefallen Sie uns damit erzeigten.

Die altdeutschen Wälder haben wir, hauptsächlich weil wir die Correctur nicht mehr selbst besorgen konnten, mit dem dritten Bande geschlossen. Wir müssen Sie daher bitten, Ihre schätzbare [sic] Beiträge solange uns zu bewahren, bis wir eine andere Zeitschrift wieder eröffnen können.

Mein Bruder empfiehlt sich mit mir Ihrem freundschaftlichen Andenken und ich bin mit der Versicherung der aufrichtigsten Hochachtung

Ew. Wohlgeb.
ergebenster
W. C. Grimm.

In his letter of July 5, 1819, Wilhelm Grimm elaborates his idea of the origin of the Nibelungen legend, an idea which is metaphysical in nature. He stresses this theory because it is an important prop for his thesis that there was an intimate relationship between Old Norse-Icelandic and old German literature. Both here and in the article in *Hermes* to which he refers, Grimm expresses the pious but subjective hope that a closer relationship between Scandinavian and German antiquity may be demonstrated.

3.
Cassel am 5ᵗᵉ Julj 1819.

Wertgeschätzter Freund,

Einen vorlaüfigen [sic] Dank für das schöne Geschenk, das Sie zu Ende des vorigen Jahres schon mir mit dem zweiten Band der Sagenbibliothek[12] gemacht, wird Ihnen meiner Bitte gemäss Hr. Prof Nyerup abgestattet haben.[13] Eine diesen Winter durch dauernde Kränklichkeit hat mich abgehalten Ihnen, wie ich wünschte, früher zu schreiben. Jetzt, nachdem ich das Werk mehrmals und sorgfältig durch gelesen sage ich Ihnen noch selbst einen grossen Dank für die vielfache Belehrung und Aufklärung die ich daraus gewonnen. Sie haben eine sehr nöthige und nützliche Aufgabe mit gewohnter Umsicht, Gelehrsamkeit und Scharfsinn gelöst, ausserdem manches neue und merkwürdige Material mitgetheilt, so dass diese Bibliothek einen dauernden Werth behält. Nachdem das Verhältnis der verschiedenartigen Ausbildungen und Darstellungen des Hauptsagenkreises besprochen und auseinandergesetzt, über die Entstehung der Wilkina Saga ein glückliches Licht verbreitet ist, kann man sich mit mehr Leichtigkeit bewegen und mit mehr Sicherheit über die Entstehung der Sage nachforschen. Ihrer Hypothese darüber, deren Scharfsinn ich anerkenne, bin ich indessen nicht zugethan.[14] Sie betrachten mir im Ganzen die Mythe zu äusserlich indem Sie ihre Entstehung von einem Zufall abhangen lassen, während ich glaube, dass die aus einer innern Nothwendigkeit hervor gegangen den Ausdruck ursprünglicher Grundanschauungen enthält. Creuzer hat darüber in den Briefen an Hermann viel treffliches gesagt.[15] Sie setzen als ersten Punct das Hervorsuchen des Erzes aus den Fluhten [sic] eines goldreichen Flusses, nun reihen sie das übrige daran, indem Sie fragen lassen: wer das Gold hineingeworfen? u. s. w. Da man ebenso gut eine andere Frage sich denken kann, etwa: wer die Feinde gewesen, vor welchen der Hort zu bergen, wen sie verfolgt hätten und dgl. so müssen Sie zugeben, dass es ein bloser Zufall ist, wenn die Sage nicht einen ganz verschiedenen Inhalt erhielt. Mir ist aber derjenige, welchen sie (jedesmal) hat, so naturnothwendig, als die Gestalt eines jeden belebten Wesens.

Ich berühre dies nur aus einem ausführlichern Urtheil, welches ich über dies wichtige Werk für die Zeitschrift Hermes abgefasst, wo Sie es in einen grössern Bericht, welcher alles, was in gegenwärtiger Zeit bei Ihnen dort für die altnordische Literatur geschehen ist, umfasst, eingewebt finden werden.[16] Bei den Kämpevisern habe ich auch einiges über unsere verschiedene Meinung von der Entstehung dieser Lieder angemerkt. Diese Abhandlung ist bestimmt Deutschland mit dem so rühmlichen und ausgezeichneten Eifer Dänemarks für diese Literatur und den neuen schätzbaren Arbeiten, die eine Folge davon sind, bekannt zu machen. Mit welcher Freude wir alles, und nun auch den zweiten Band der Edda empfangen,[17] brauche ich Ihnen nicht zu sagen. Die Verbindung der dänischen und deutschen Literatur wird immer genauer und das Verhältnis zwischen beiden vertraulicher und freundlicher werden, wie es der Natur der Sache angemessen ist; hoffentlich glückt es auch noch, eine nähere Verwandtschaft der eddischen Lieder mit der ältesten deutschen Poesie nachzuweisen.

Mein Bruder empfiehlt sich mit mir Ihrem fernern freundschaftlichen Andenken, das uns sehr werth ist. M [it] der Versicherung der aufrichtigsten Hochschätzung.

Ganz der Ihrige
W. C. Grimm.

Wilhelm Grimm's letter of February 11, 1824, bespeaks his active interest in runology during the third decade of the nineteenth century. He was first and foremost concerned with trying to prove that there were German runes as distinct from Scandinavian runes. In 1821 he published *Über deutsche Runen;* in 1828 he published a supplementary article on runes in the *Wiener Jahrbücher.* The article discussed in detail the codices and other evidence mentioned in his letter.

P. E. Müller's dedication of his book to Wilhelm Grimm must have been bittersweet to Grimm, for he had to share this honor with Friedrich David Gräter and Friedrich Heinrich von der Hagen, with neither of whom the Grimm brothers were on good terms. Gräter, champion of Scandinavian antiquities in Germany from 1789 until his death in 1830, had long corresponded with Müller and other Danish scholars before the Grimms became interested in Scandinavia; he could not reconcile himself to the eminent position the Grimms so quickly assumed in the field of Germanic philology and the Grimms thought him to be conceited and unco-operative. As aforementioned, von der Hagen vied with the Grimms to be the first to publish the text and a translation of the so-called Elder Edda in Germany.

The "Goldhörner" to which Grimm refers are of course the golden horns of Gallehus. P. E. Müller had written about them in 1806 in *Antikvarisk Undersøgelese om de ved Gallehuus fundne Guldhorne,* which had been published as a prize essay by the Royal Danish Academy. The age and origin of the golden horns are still a matter of dispute. Whether they depict Scandinavian, Celtic, or some other mythology or legend is conjecture.

4.

Cassel 11te Febr. 1824.

Hochgeschätzter Freund,

Ihr bereits am 20.[n] August v. J. geschriebener Brief, und das Buch,[18] welches er begleitete, sind erst vor kurzem in meine Hände gelangt und das ist Schuld, dass meine Antwort so spät erscheint. Sie haben mir eine grosse Freude gemacht, sowohl durch Ihre gelehrte und belehrende Schrift, als durch die Zueignung derselben, die ich zu verdienen wünsche und wofür ich Ihnen auf das herzlichste danke.[19] Besondern Werth setze ich in das nähere und freundliche Verhältnis der dänischen und deutschen Litteratur, das allmählig eingetreten ist, eine Verbindung, die ich zu allen Zeiten gewünscht und nach meinen geringen Kräften befördert habe. Seitdem ich die Überschrift der altnordischen Litteratur in den Hermes geliefert habe ist wieder eine Reihe schätzbare Werke bei Ihnen erschienen und ich denke ernstlich an eine Fortsetzung jener Abhandlung; fürs erste habe ich von Ihrer Schrift einen Bericht für die Göttinger Anzeigen geschrieben,[20] wozu ich umso mehr mich veranlasst fühlte, als ich schon früher die Untersuchung über Snorres Quellen dort angezeigt hatte.[21] Ich stimme Ihrem Urtheil über Saxo im Ganzen bei, vielleicht würde ich dem mythischen hier und da mehr Werth an und für sich und weniger in Beziehung auf die Geschichte beilegen, aber ich glaube dass nur auf dem Weg den Sie einschlagen, wo jeder einzelnen Sage ihr Recht widerfährt und jede für sich behandelt wird, ein wahres und fruchtbares Urtheil über den Saxo sich bilden kann. Nur gehört dazu so viel Scharfsinn und Gelehrsamkeit, als Sie besitzen. Dahlmann[22] haben Sie sehr gut widerlegt, so weil er in seiner Abhandlung von Wahrheit und Unbefangenheit spricht, so gefällt er sich doch selbst zu sehr in der witzigen Manier und in den behenden Sprüngen, womit er des (in seinem Irrthum doch immer schuldlosen) Saxos Nichtigkeit aufzudecken glaubt.

Das periculum runologicum von Brynjulf[23] ist allerdings in meinen Händen, so wie die viel unbedeutendere Schrift von Bredsdorf.[24] Jene genau zu prüfen werde ich vollkommen Anlass haben, wenn ich einen Nachtrag zu meiner Schrift über deutsche Runen ausarbeite. Ausser genauere Durchzeichnungen der S^t

Galler Alphabete,[25] wozu noch ein paar runische Worte kommen, die verblichen waren und erst durch den Gebrauch chemischer Mittel hervorgetreten sind, habe ich noch zwei ganz neu entdeckte Runenalphabete erhalten, wovon das eine in einem Salzburger Codex des 10ⁿ Jahrh. das andere in einem Vaticanischen des 11.ⁿ Jahrh. ist gefunden worden.[26] Ich warte aber noch auf genauere Nachrichten und Abzeichnungen von Ihren dortigen Goldbrachteaten, eher mag ich nicht ans Werk gehen. Auch Liljegrens Abhandlung, die doch gerühmt wird, entbehre ich noch.[27] Unser Palæograph Kopp[28] hat, wie er mir schon vor einem Jahr erzählte, eine Abhandlung über den Ursprung der Runen fertig, worin er die alte Meinung vertheidigen will, dass sie nur ein verderbtes runisches Alphabet seyen, also ein Gegner, aber bei seinem natürlichen Scharfsinn und der grossen Gelehrsamkeit in seinem Fache ein sehr achtungswürdiger Feind. So viel ist gewiss, dass auch die Runenlitteratur sich neu belebt hat.

Was die beiden Goldhörner betrifft,[29] so muss ich bekennen, dass ich nicht Ihrer Meinung bin, das habe ich Nyerup schon mündtlich geäussert, als er uns vor ein paar Jahren besuchte, und dass ich kein anderes als das angelsächsisch-deutsche Runenalphabet darin erkennen könnte; in meiner Schrift hatte ich deshalb ganz geschwiegen, weil ich glaubte, dass Ihre sorgfältige und gelehrte Arbeit eine besondere Widerlegung verlangte. Das Wort HORNA [in runes] (HORNO bei Brynjulf ist falsch) war mir gleich anfangs ausser Zweifel; bis ietzt bin ich auch nicht geneigt, den beiden Hörnern ein hohes Alter beizulegen.

Mein Bruder der fleissig an dem 2n Bande seiner Grammatik, von welchem schon einige Bogen gedruckt sind, arbeit [*sic*] empfiehlt sich Ihnen angelegentlich. Schenken Sie uns ferner Ihr Wohlwollen und Freundschaft; mit aufrichtiger Hochachtung und Ergebenheit.

der Ihrige Wilhelm C. Grimm.

Wilhelm Grimm's last letter to P. E. Müller, written September 11, 1829, accompanied a copy of *Die deutsche Heldensage* (Göttingen, 1829). While praising the *Sagabibliothek* in his foreword, Grimm expressly disagreed with P. E. Müller and professed of the several Eddic lays discussed in *Die deutsche Heldensage*: "Ich gebe diesen eddischen Liedern unter den Zeugnissen für die einheimische Saga einen Platz, weil nach meiner Ueberzeugung ihr Grundstoff deutsch ist" (p. 4). P. E. Müller replied June 28, 1830, and expressed his thanks for the copy of Wilhelm Grimm's book, but did not enter into a further discussion of the national origins of the Eddic lays. His letter is printed in *Briefwechsel*, pp. 143-144. This was the end of the correspondence between Wilhelm Grimm and P. E. Müller. Müller became Bishop of Zealand in 1830 and was subsequently less able to devote time to scholarly pursuits. He died in 1834.

The letter of introduction from P. E. Müller to Wilhelm Grimm printed in *Briefwechsel,* pp. 142-143, is incorrectly dated by Ernst Schmidt. As may be concluded from the dates of publication of the books mentioned, the letter was written in 1821 and not in 1829.

5.

Cassel 11 Septbr 1829

Hierbei, verehrtester Freund, übersende ich Ihnen eine so eben fertig gewordene Schrift, welche die Grundlage einer Geschichte der deutschen Heldensage liefert, in der Hoffnung, dass der Gegenstand selbst noch immer im Stande ist Ihre Theilnahme zu erregen. Was und wieviel ich Ihrer Sagenbibliothek bei Beurtheilung der nordischen Denkmäler verdanke, habe ich deutlich ausgesprochen, wenn ich in einigen Stücken von Ihrer Ansicht abweiche, so wird Ihnen dies bei Ihrer Neigung zu freier, unbefangener Forschung, eher willkommen, als unange nem seyn. Ich habe bei der Untersuchung über den Inhalt der Fabel selbst einen andern Weg versucht; ich möchte gerne erst den aus mannigfachen Gründen eingetretenen Veränderungen auf die Spur kommen und zu dem, was ich ursprünglich nenne, gelangt seyn, bevor ich einen Versuch machte, den Sinn und Gedanken der Sage zu errathen.

Ich erlaube mir zugleich einen besondern Abdruck einer Abhandlung über Runen beizulegen.[30] Bei uns ist so eben ein Werk von Hr Legis über diesen Gegenstand erschienen,[31] welcher auch angefangen hat die ältere Edda zu übersetzen;[32] doch scheint er mir bis ietzt mehr fleissige Zusammenstellungen, als neue Untersuchungen zu liefern. Erfreulich ist aber die Bemerkung, dass die nordische Literatur immer fester bei uns wurzelt.

Wie sehr dankbar ich Ihnen und dem Arnamag. Institut für die überschickten höchst schätzbaren und trefflichen Werke[33] bin, brauche ich Ihnen wohl nicht erst auszudrucken; Sie sind davon überzeugt. Von dem dritten Bande der Edda habe ich eine Anzeige in die Göttinger gelehrte Blätter geschickt.[34] welche meine Landesleute einlädt diese nun vollständig eröffneten Quellen nach ihrem Werthe zu erkennen und zu benutzen.

Die Einlage an Hn Prof. Finn Magnussen und Hn Staatsrath Thorlacius haben Sie wohl die Güte, abgeben zu lassen.[35] Wie leid thut es mir, dem guten Nyerup nichts mehr mitsenden zu können.[36]

Ich kehre ietzt wieder zu einer Bearbeitung des Freidank zurück, wozu ich sehr reichliche Materialen gesammelt habe.[37] Er fällt in das erste Viertel des 13ten Jahrh. und ist ein merkwürdiger Denkmal für die Bildung und den Geist jener Zeit, die an feiner Betrachtung des Lebens der unsrigen kaum nachsteht.

Ihrem ferneren freundschaftlichen Andenken empfehle ich mich angelegentlich, seyn Sie überzeugt, dass ich es sehr hochschätze und Ihrer allzeit mit der aufrichtigsten Verehrung gedenke

Wilh. Grimm.

REFERENCES

1. Christian Hinrich Wolke, 1741-1825.
2. *Om det islandske Sprogs Vigtighed. Et af det kongelige Selskab for Norges Vel kronet Prisskrift,* Kiøbenhavn, 1813.
3. *Ueber den Ursprung und Verfall der isländischen Historiographie,* ... Kopenhagen, 1813.
4. *Udvalgte Danske Viser fra Middelalderen; efter A. S. Vedels og P. Syvs trykte Udgaver og efter haandskrevne Samlinger udgivne paa ny af Abrahamson, Nyerup og Rahbek,* I-V, Kjøbenhavn, 1812-1814.
5. Anders Sørensen Vedel's *Et Hundrede danske Viser* was published in 1591; in 1695 Peder Syv republished Vedel's collection augmented by 100 more folksongs.
6. *Altdänische Heldenlieder, Balladen und Märchen. Übersetzt von Wilhelm Carl Grimm,* Heidelberg, 1811.
7. The reference is to the fifth volume of *Udvalgte danske Viser fra Middelalderen,* ... [1812] 1814.
8. *Lieder der alten Edda. Aus der Handschrift herausgegeben und erklärt durch die Brüder Grimm. I. Band.,* Berlin, 1815.
9. *Der arme Heinrich aus der Strassburgischen und Vatikanischen Hs., erklärt durch die Gebrüder Grimm,* Berlin, 1815.
10. Georg Andreas Reimer, 1776-1842, the well-known publisher and bookseller.
11. I. e., the Arna-Magnæan Commission.
12. I. e., Volume II of the Danish edition, published in Copenhagen in 1818.
13. In a letter to Nyerup dated August 28, 1818, Wilhelm Grimm had sent greetings to P. E. Müller and remarked, "Ich freue mich sehr auf den zweiten Band seiner Sagenbibliothek." (*Briefwechsel,* p. 79.)
14. On page 20 of the volume in question Müller concluded: "At jo tydeligere en Saga bærer Præg af ren digterisk Oprindelse, jo rimeligere dens Ælde. Det poetiske Præg viser sig baade i Indholdet og Foredraget." Grimm does not reply directly to Müller's ideas.
15. *Briefe über Homer und Hesiodus vorzüglich über die Theogonie von Gottfried Hermann und Friedrich Creuzer,* ... Heidelberg, 1818.
16. "Die altnordische Literatur in der gegenwärtigen Periode" in *Hermes oder kritisches Jahrbuch der Literatur* ... 1820, Nr. V der ganzen Folge, pp. 1-53. Repr. in *Kleinere Schriften* von Wilhelm Grimm, III, 1-84.
17. Volume II of the Arna-Magnæan Commission's edition of the Elder Edda was published in 1818.
18. Peter Erasmus Müller, *Critisk Undersøgelse af Danmarks og Norges Sagnhistorie eller om Troværdigheden af Saxos og Snorros Kilder ... Særskilt aftrykt af det kongelige danske Videnskabernes Selskabs Skrifter,* Kiöbenhavn, 1823.
19. The work was dedicated: "De trende Hædersmænd: den nordiske Oldtids Lærde Kiendere i Tydskland, F. O. [sic] Gräter, W. C. Grimm, F. H. von der Hagen ...."
20. *Göttingische gelehrte Anzeigen,* I, 11 März 1824, 410-410. Repr. in *Kleinere Schriften,* II, pp. 294-302.
21. *Ibid.,* III, 1 October 1821, 1561-1566. Reprinted in *Kleinere Schriften,* II, 279-283.

WILHELM GRIMM'S LETTERS TO PETER ERASMUS MÜLLER

22. F. C. Dahlmann, "Einleitung in die Geschichte von Alt-Dänemark" in *Forschungen auf dem Gebiete der Geschichte, I,* Altona, 1822. Dahlmann ascribed no historical worth to Saxo.

23. Gísli Brynjúlfsson, *Periculum runologicum. Dissertatio inauguralis* . . . Havniæ, 1823. With Bredsdorff's *Om Runeskriftens Oprindelse,* reviewed by Wilhelm Grimm in *Göttingische gelehrte Anzeigen,* II, 26 Juni 1824, 1017-1032; repr. in *Kleinere Schriften,* II, 324-337. Reviewed by P. E. Müller in *Dansk Litteratur Tidende,* 1823, pp. 741-746.

24. Jakob Hornemann Bresdorff, *Om Runeskriftens Oprindelse,* Kjöbenhavn, 1822 (pp. 19+1 pl.). Reviewed by P. E. Müller in *Dansk Litteratur Tidende,* 1823, pp. 725-729; Bredsdorff replied to Müller in a supplement to the same periodical, 1823. Bredsdorff criticized Wilhelm Grimm in "Om de saakaldte tydske Runer; eller Bemærkninger ved W. C. Grimms Skrift 'Über deutsche Runen' in *Nordisk Tidsskrift for Historie, Literatur og Konst,* II, 1828, 394-403.

25. These alphabets, from the St. Gall codices 270 and 878, are reproduced in table II, accompanying Wilhelm Grimm's *Ueber deutsche Runen,* Göttingen, 1821.

26. Identified by Grimm in the *Wiener Jahrbücher,* 1828, as Bibl. Christ. Vatic. 338, Fol. 90, and membrana Salisburgiensis No. 140, preserved in Vienna.

27. Johan Gustaf Liljegren, "Anteckningar rörande versar, skrefne med Runor" in *Det Skandinaviske Literatur Selskabs Skrifter,* XVII, 1820, 374-420.

28. Ulrich Friedrich Kopp (1762-1834), the author of *Palaegraphia critica,* I-IV, 1817-1829.

29. P. E. Müller's *Antivarisk Undersøgelse over de ved Gallehuus fundne, Guldhorne. Et af Videnskabernes Selskab i Kiöbenhavn kronet Prisskrift* was published in 1806. It was also published in German translation the same year.

30. *Zur Literatur der Runen. Nebst Mittheilung runischer Alphabete und gothischer Fragmente aus Handschriften . . . (Aus dem XLIII. Bande der Wiener Jahrbücher der Literatur besonders abgedruckt),* Wien, 1828.

31. Gustav Thormod Legis, i.e., G. T. Glückselig, *Die Runen und ihre Denkmäler,* Leipzig, 1829.

32. Gustav Thormod Legis, *Edda, die Stammmutter der Poesie und der Weisheit des Nordens. Lyrisch-epische Dichtungen, Mythen und Sagen der Gotho-Germanischen Vorzeit. Zum erstenmal aus der isländischen Urschrift übertragen, mit ästhetisch-kritischen Bemerkungen, mythologischen Erläuterungen, einem fortlaufendem Commentar und Register versehen. Erste* [only] *Abtheilung. Mit einer kosmologischen Karte,* Leipzig, 1829.—Despite the boastful title, the book is nothing but a plagiarism of part of Finnur Magnusson's *Den ældre Edda,* . . . Kjøbenhavn, 1821-1823.

33. Including volume III of the Commission's edition of the Elder Edda.

34. *Göttingische gelehrte Anzeigen,* III, 26 September 1829, 1557-1559. Reprinted in *Kleinere Schriften,* II, 396-397.

35. Finnur Magnússon's reply to Grimm's letter of September 4, 1829, is printed in *Briefwechsel,* pp. 203-206. The Icelandic scholar thanked Grimm for "Deres unique Skrift 'über die deutsche Heldensage' und instructive Afhandlung om Runerne . . . ." I have been unable to locate Grimm's letter to Finnur Magnússon or to Børge Thorlacius.

36. Nyerup died in June 1829.

37. Wilhelm Grimm's edition, *Vrídankes Bescheidenheit,* was published in Göttingen in 1834.

[137]

The Problem of Catholic Sympathies in Swedish Romanticism

ADOLPH B. BENSON

Yale University

LITERARY HISTORIANS have agreed that there were, in general, two principal groups of writers in Swedish Romanticism: the so-called Gothic School, which in its activities favored national or patriotic themes; and the more philosophical New Romanticists or New School, whose members—all young—sought guidance and inspiration from Germany. The latter were known as Phosphorists, after their publication *Phosphoros*, and ardently studied Novalis, Fichte, Schelling, Tieck, the Brothers Schlegel, Werner, Fouqué, and Wackenroder. Also, in imitation of these German authors, they plunged enthusiastically into the literature of the Catholic, south European poets—Ariosto, Dante, Petrarch, Tasso, Calderon, and Cervantes. The Phosphorists, headed by P. D. A. Atterbom (1790-1855), Lorenzo Hammarskjöld (1785-1827), and Wilhelm Fredrik Palmblad (1788-1852), were interested not only in the philosophical background of their German models but in their socially and politically reactionary program—their worship of the Middle Ages, and their logical sympathies for the medieval religion, Catholicism.

In Germany the Catholicizing tendencies among the Romanticists—most of whom originally were Protestants—proved very serious indeed, from an orthodox viewpoint, and several German writers, such as Friedrich Schlegel, Count F. L. von Stolberg, and Zacharias Werner, joined the Catholic Church. What would be the results in Sweden among the Phosphorists, who idealized their German masters and their philosophy, but were, all of them, members of the Swedish State Church, which was exclusively Lutheran? There were Catholic churches in Sweden at the time, primarily for Catholic foreigners and members of the foreign diplomatic corps; but what were the native Swedish Romanticists to do if they decided to follow religiously the gospel of the Germans? No matter what their Catholic sympathies might be, they were, under the existing Swedish laws of about 1810, liable to be exiled if they formally joined the Catholic Church. Did they join it? If not, did they either privately or publicly acclaim their Catholic sympathies, if any?

In answer to queries in the matter we find the greatest possible variation of opinions among critics and literary mentors. They differ about the very existence of such sympathies, and those who concede that there were some vary considerably in their ideas about the character, importance, and distribution method of the Catholicizing propaganda. Apparently, as we shall see later, a few sensitive, orthodox Protestant Swedes at the beginning of the last century actually believed that the Phosphoristic youngsters intended to reintroduce Catholicism into Sweden; yet Karl Warburg, as late as 1913, claims[1] that the new religiosity so common among the young German Romanticists lacked in Sweden, where it was imitated, "all Catholic tendencies." E. N. Tigerstedt likewise fails, in 1948, to find any real counterpart (*verklig motsvarighet*) in Swedish letters to "that religion of beauty or Catholicizing enthusiasm which plays such a large role abroad."[2] Which judgment is correct? Even Tigerstedt, however, admits an *ansats*, a beginning, of a Catholic *svärmeri*. This paper is an attempt to reopen a problem, now almost forgotten, to present the obvious evidence in the case, and obtain some form of a reasonable verdict. Obviously, the results cannot be exhaustive, but even so we shall discover that the truth lies somewhere between the two extremes.

[139]

THE PROBLEM OF CATHOLIC SYMPATHIES IN SWEDISH ROMANTICISM

Aside from first-hand observations of original works made by the writer while gathering material for his dissertation on another topic of Swedish Romanticism,[3] the chief reason for this brief but long-contemplated study is the post-Romantic criticism of the New School, which, often violent, included bitter attacks on the Phosphorists' attitude toward Catholicism. Where there is so much smoke there must be some fire; so we shall first examine this testimony, the importance of which lies in the fact that most of it appeared many years after the polemic battle between the Old and New School was over, when we might expect from it some objectivity and sane afterthought. These qualities do not always appear, to be sure, but whether or not in their discussions the critics and historians are prejudiced, some semblance to the facts will to an observant reader emerge from their writings.

A sworn enemy of the New Romanticists was Anders Fryxell, who in his *Bidrag*[4] collected and recorded all anti-Romantic material that he could find. He said it was the fashion among the Romanticists in general to speak ill of Luther and Protestantism and lean toward obscurantism and the Catholic *fides implicita*.[5] Basing his contention on articles in the anti-Romanticist *Allmänna Journalen* for 1816 and 1817, which was contemporaneous with the polemic culmination of the Romantic revolt, he pretends to show that the Phosphorists' Christianity was against the State Church and full of contradictions and absurdities. "Here [in these articles of the opposition] it appeared in...an indisputable way," says Fryxell, "that the Phosphorists revealed a not insignificant sympathy for various Catholic views."[6] Furthermore, the critic resuscitates, quite naturally, Esaias Tegnér's well-known derogatory references to the Phosphorists, especially the accusation in *Nyåret 1816* ("New Year 1816") that their religion was Jesuit, containing the now famous ironic, ridiculing verse: "Long live the Pope—and Old Nick!"[7] Only occasionally, says Fryxell, do we in Phosphoristic circles detect an honest acceptance of the teachings of Protestantism. More often it is either a symbolism à la Schelling, or a semi-Catholic mysticism. He feels that the faith of the Phosphorists is dangerous to the Lutheran faith.[8] The author goes into the religious aspects of Romanticism very seriously and at great length. Though narrow in his ideas perhaps, he is sincere and somewhat concerned. He accuses the Romantic rebels of placing Catholic tradition above the Bible, and while there was not among the Phosphorists, in so many words, he admits, any definite preference for the Roman faith, it was nevertheless favored in an indirect way, "namely through all manners of speech and illusions akin to it," and, he adds, "of the Holy Virgin there was a wellnigh Catholic idolatry."[9] Most of these assertions are essentially correct, as we shall soon see, but it might be mentioned at once in anticipation that for some obscure causes the religious ravings of the Phosphorists did not at any time prove really dangerous to the Lutheran Church, and that may be one reason why some modern critics refuse to believe that there ever had been any Catholic sympathy in the first place. Was it on the part of the State Church a case of mere patience, condescension, and tolerance, just silently watching its sinning offspring until it got over its youthful whims?

Fryxell in his attack struck at one undeniable fact in the philosophy of the New Romanticists—their adulation for the Holy Virgin, and the leading Phosphorists in this respect were no exceptions. Mary became the intermediary agent between heaven and earth, and her love, apparently, the only link between the two. Seldom is Christ mentioned in Swedish Romantic poetry and polemics without His mother. She occupies the seat in heaven nearest God's throne, and Atterbom speaks of "the time when all hearts should beat for Christus and Maria."[10] Mary is the *Urbild* among women, the original model of beauty, piety, and motherliness, especially after she had become a historical figure and as world queen had been placed on a heavenly throne. "This mother of love," says Atterbom, 1821, "has not even today, under this name, been forgotten in southern Europe."[11]

A typical, significant, historico-philosophical concept of the Holy Virgin (quoted in part by Fryxell) is found in Atterbom's introduction (*Företal*) to *Poetisk Kalender* for 1816. A few lines of the original will to readers of Scandinavian languages best illustrate both form and content:

> När urbilden af förnuftets och försynens verldsordning såsom sådan vid Kristi födelse antog historisk individualitet, framträdde och i Försonarns moder den historiska gestalten af naturens försonade själ, skönhetens eviga oskuld, (virgo mater, ex *spiritu* concipiens) och i glorian af qvinlighetens högsta förklaring, den moderliga ömheten, vördades hon af Sonens församling såsom en mild förmedlarinna mellan hans oupphinneliga helighet och det bräckliga jordelifvets förvillelser....

In substance: when Christ at birth assumed historic personality, there appeared also, in the Redeemer's mother, the historic form of the redeemed soul of nature, who as the personification of "the eternal beauty of innocence" and motherly tenderness was revered by "the Son's congregation" (humanity) as an intermediator between "His sanctity and the errors of the earth." The general idea, despite the misty phraseology, is tolerably clear. Mary is the symbol of nature; and, furthermore, her Son is the *Urbild* of reason, who had taken on mortality but later returned to His original state. Nature is not God's personality, according to Atterbom but (through it) God expresses himself in human form. It is, as Albert Nilsson has pointed out,[12] the Schelling-New-Platonic atonement concept. The Christian Mary represents the Egyptian Isis, the Ephesian Diana, and the Scandinavian Freja and Frigga. Also, Mary and the Christ child *together* represent the *eternal nature*; in fact, they *together* redeem heaven and earth, and Mary follows her Son back to His divine origin—if the present writer understands the idea correctly. At all events, the Holy Virgin is the central figure in Atterbom's nature philosophy. When in Germany on his way to Italy, 1817, he penned in German his conception of the Mother of Jesus as "eternal nature" in a poetic cycle of several sonnets, *Maria, Die Mutter Gottes.* Three historical periods are represented in these sonnets: those of nature (the Golden Age), the tragic Fall (from nature), and Christianity, with a demand for redemption. The fourth sonnet reveals the reconciliation between nature and spirit, through Jesus becoming man. The Divine Child is the fruit of the union of light and pure nature (Mary).

Certainly this attention to the Holy Virgin, even though chiefly poetic and philosophic, was a little unusual for a Lutheran and could easily at the time have been misinterpreted. As for Catholicism in general, the New School in Sweden professed to believe that "a more perfect form of Christian revelation could hardly in the beginning have been imagined. . . ."[13] The Pope could with good reason have himself acclaimed as God's vicar on earth, because he really was that, according to the idea prevailing during this [initial] period of development." Moreover, the New School, as Fryxell mentions, had accused the Protestants of a "much greater fanaticism than the one which they fought [against Catholics] when they in a "cloud of abuses concealed the majestic form of Catholicism.""[14] The Reformation was negative, said the Romanticists, and its "chemical reason-process," whatever the exact meaning may be, had been dissolved into a "complete decomposition of all its constituents." Its purpose was to "destroy the external spiritual authority, the Church, because a trail was to be blazed for the inner, higher one, reason's own."[15] There should on the part of the younger generation be more sympathy for the Middle Ages.—Surely, we find here a phase of definite Catholic sympathies.

Bernhard Elis Malmström published in 1868 a whole volume dealing with the controversy between the Old and the New School.[16] He has no great love for the Romanticists either, but is a little more sensible and moderate in his condemnations. He has, of course, discovered Atterbom's sympathy for the Middle Ages and the Holy Virgin, but believes that this "Catholic digression" was more of the imagination than of the heart, and that the "Mariakult" was but a speech form adopted from his "Romantic-Catholic models."[17] Maybe so. Yet he admits that this Catholicizing digression had in its day caused strong misgivings among the public against him [Atterbom] and his School. Women and children were the most affected, says Malmström, but we cannot help wondering how much the women and children in general could possibly have known about the New School and its frequently obscure gospels. The author is inconsistent. Catholic tendencies are in one place seemingly denied, and still he concedes at the same time that there are grounds for their existence. But he points out that young men (New Romanticists, probably) did not have sufficient experience in religious dogmas to realize that the "combination of Christ and Mary really signified the recognition of a Catholic article of faith."[18] It could not, he says, be explained away by any reference to the motherly principle in nature; and, moreover, in Germany the Mary cult had become something more than a poetic, esthetic, or philosophic manner of speech. In other words, the author recognizes at least a superficial, though possibly unconscious, Catholic influence. Malmström is no friend of the Catholic Church and berates the New School for urging tolerance of intolerance itself as objectified in the Catholic organization. (We shall return to this subject later.) The critic includes, from *Allmänna Journalen* for

1817, the Old School's attack on the New one for its Catholicism and monkery, for its alleged belittlement of the Lutheran Reformation, and its defense of hierarchal principles, superstition, and folk beliefs.

Malmström devotes several pages to a description of Phosphoristic views on religion. He describes how the New School in its journals reviewed favorably any critical or literary works that were friendly to Catholicism and handled severely those that were not.[19] And the favoritism was not a momentary feeling but a conviction. The Phosphorists had suggested a translation, into Swedish presumably, of Stolberg's *Geschichte der Kristus-Religion*, which was so strong for Catholicism that it claimed Peter was a bishop in Rome. Malmström examined the Romantic *Svensk Litteratur-Tidning* for 1814 very thoroughly and found that the Middle Ages and its spirit, including the Papal power, were lauded at every opportunity: the medieval era was one with a definite form of life; it was an age of deep religiosity, honest faith, brave deeds, and knightly honor. The Reformation lacked all these. The Papal rule symbolized the power which reason should exercise over brute force; whereas the Reformation, after removing the obstructions to science, art, and religion, would have to end by removing itself, as the most serious hindrance,[20] a statement the latter part of which is clear only in its unfavorable attitude toward the Reformation. It was Catholicism which held Christianity together before Luther and was the foundation of its culture, the New School had declared.

The most flagrant charge perhaps against the New Romanticists was their alleged defense of "intolerance and persecution" [as supposedly practiced by Catholics] in religious matters. In *Svensk Litteratur-Tidning* for 1815 (No. 8) they had claimed that an ecclesiastical state (such as the Catholic Church, presumably) had the same right, through any legitimate means avail-

THE PROBLEM OF CATHOLIC SYMPATHIES IN SWEDISH ROMANTICISM

able, to defend itself against heresy as a political one might, from traitors. This resulted in a sharp rejoinder from Malmström, and in connection with another phase of the subject he quotes from an opposition article to the effect that there were no Jesuits in Sweden to start trouble between the regent and his subjects, no inquisition courts, and no undesirable prelates. Nor were there any people who longed for the bosom of Catholicism.—Obviously, the whole tone of Malmström's critical report, like that of Fryxell, assumes the presence of noticeable Catholic tendencies among the Phosphorists, call them what you will.

Apropos of the Holy Virgin cult and other religious affairs Palmblad in 1818[21] had made a farewell defense plea for the views of the New School, a plea that was duly reported by Malmström in his volume. It was perfectly proper, Palmblad had said, to revere, though not to worship, the Mother of Christ, and none should be called a papist for the exercise of that reverence. She was, after all, the mediator (between man and her Son). But of course, said the defendant, the chief critic of the opposition (the editor of *Allmänna Journalen*, P. A. Wallmark), would not understand that. Only an artist or poet would, and Wallmark was neither, according to Palmblad. The members of the New School had been called Schellingians, atheists, Catholics, pantheists, New-Platonists, and Swedenborgians, so that name-calling meant nothing. The reasons why he had praised the Middle Ages, he continued, was that others had not in their attitudes been reasonable toward the period, and every era had both its good and bad features. Were not the Middle Ages the roots of the present? A single, powerful head of the church at that time was desirable, because it was necessary. He accused the opposition of ignorance, and suggested that much of the prattle about tolerance was but another name for indifference toward things holy. Palmblad presented a historical viewpoint which was relatively fair and moderate, although the present writer cannot always follow his arguments on Luther.

In connection with Palmblad and Malmström, it might be mentioned here that the latter had in Part 4 of his *Grunddragen*[22] severely criticized the former's translation of Cervantes' "Hymn to the Holy Virgin," 1810. He is not sure, he says, whether the translation was done for the Holy Virgin or for poetry; in any event, it is worthless and no honor to poetry. Palmblad's friend Hammarskjöld had, to be sure, he continues, reviewed it favorably in *Polyfem* (a polemic journal of the Phosphorists) for July 24, 1811, but then he was obliged to, following a "Jesuitical morality" of untruth.—Cervantes' "Hymn" had also in Germany been translated by A. W. Schlegel, and it was by some critics believed that Palmblad had in his rendering used the German version. Malmström's criticism was purely metrical and poetic, not religious.

Malmström attacks in the same volume[23] the Swedish Romanticists' attitude toward charity, which, he implies, is that of the Catholic countries. Good works, according to the New School, should arise from personal compassion, pity, and sympathy; hence aid should come exclusively from individual acts of mercy, rather than public. There should be no poor tax, for example, no joint community effort as such. This method does not work, says Malmström; under it both the individual and the community as a whole would suffer. The social order would be disturbed by the system of free beggary. Just look at the Catholic countries. No, it is better for the poor to get something by law rather than be humiliated by private gifts. Duty, not sentimentality, is the basis of public aid. And public charity is not made indispensable through an occasional rich man's gift. We need more than the casting of a coin to a beggar who will rush to a saloon to spend it.—Here most of us will, at least in part, agree with Malmström.

A more factual, objective, and interpretative criticism of the New School appeared in 1873-1895, when Gustaf Ljunggren published his monumental *Svenska Vitterhetens Häfder*.[24] He readily acknowledges the Phosphorists' enthusiasm for the Middle Ages and Catholicism, but it was, he believes, a purely esthetic tendency.[25] The religion of the New School was, he explains, a "productive" one, à la Novalis and Schleiermacher, and the most important German influences had been Tieck's *Genoveva* and *Kaiser Octavianus,* with its medieval atmosphere of legends and miracles. Moreover, the Swedish Romantic leaders had been anxious to establish the identity of poetry and religion, and in Atterbom's address at his initiation into the society Musis Amici, October 7, 1807, he had stressed this identity and in the very middle of his speech had inserted a sonnet to the Holy Virgin. In a similar address to Auroraförbundet he had asserted in substance: The history of Jesus is the *highest poetry*, a reunion between heaven and earth. The Holy Virgin is the symbol of poetry; her Son, that of religion; and there are only a few noble souls, such as Jesus's disciples, who in childish innocence follow their teachings [i.e. of Mary and her Son] and guided by a pious *aning* and a sorrow-free faith, "gambol" (*leka sig*) into heaven.[26] Georg Ingelgren, a minor friend and member of the Romantic group, in commenting upon Atterbom's poem "The Churchyard" (*Kyrkogården*), says it is wholly "mystic and betrays the leanings of the younger members toward Catholicism." "I do not wish to maintain," he continues, "that one must be a Catholic to be a good poet; but it is undeniable that Catholicism is highly poetic. The Madonna, the beautiful ideal of womanly perfection, animates true inspiration."[27] Ljunggren knows that in Germany Novalis's *Die Christenheit und Europa* had caused many to join the Catholic Church; but the Swedish Romanticists had not been so radical, he avers—not so far as *action* is concerned. They had rather followed the method of Tieck and A. W. Schlegel [who did not formally become Catholics]. Hence it was all a *prédilection d'artiste*.[28] Yet, these Swedes had cast longing glances in the Catholic direction, he admits, with all its cult, legends, martyrs, and sense of beauty. They had admired the hierarchical structure of the Catholic Church; but "only the worship of Mary seems to have been [especially] desirable to them; and they come back to her often in speech and writing, and seldom name the Savior without speaking of the Mother."[29]

It is now well known, from their published correspondence, that Atterbom and Hammarskjöld in particular had in their early days been much impressed by visits to a Catholic church. Atterbom, in 1810, still had vivid memories of his visit to one five years before; and Hammarskjöld in a letter to his colleague Claes Livijn, of September 3, 1809, writes that if he were not married he might some fine day "Stolbergerize," i.e., turn Catholic like Count L. von Stolberg, who in 1800, with most of his family, had gone over to the Catholic faith. Also, in a letter to Carl Christoffer Gjörwell of March 12, 1808, Hammarskjöld had expressed enthusiasm for a certain copy of Raphael's Madonna and Child. Mary's figure, said the writer, had so much beauty that she was fitted to be the mother of a god. But this, opines Ljunggren, is but an expression of Hammarskjöld's love for "external symbolism." His religion was esthetic, and he speaks of Christ as one who like Socrates preached with word and example the highest form of morality. He had maintained that Greek paganism and Catholicism were perfect means for displaying the powers of imagination. As for Atterbom, he had in the above-mentioned address to the Musis Amici, on "Religion's Inseparable Relation to Poetry," pictured an antique "Gothic temple, with all of its

Catholic cult and had apotheosized the poetic dogmas of Catholicism, whereupon there had followed the omnipresent sonnet to Mary, already noted. It was followed by other poems in the same mood. In *Phosphoros* for 1810, in "The Christmas Matins" (*Julottan*), the image of Mary appears and definitely gives a friendly nod to the poet. In a review on art, in the last number of Phosphoros, 1813, Atterbom proclaims in enthusiastic language that painters have never painted anything higher than the Mother of God, the eternally heavenly Virgin, and her Son, out of whose eyes shines a supernatural splendor that expresses the contents of all Christianity.[30] In the same number, also, there appears in verse a rather fantastic story, "Helga Ragnhild," of two pious nuns, one of whom, in a castle, runs into the customary trouble with a troll or erlking. The legend has an abundance of fire, angels, miracles; and a point of the Cross opens a wall to the nuns when most needed. Ljunggren is not sure that the poet himself believed it. The author was Palmblad, who, incidentally, had on August 21, 1808, written to Atterbom about possible translations of some German dramas: *Die Jungfrau von Orleans, Die Söhne des Thals,* and *Genoveva,* by Schiller, Werner, and Tieck, respectively, all of which had the desired background. Palmblad said he liked them all and in deep devotion knelt before them.

Illuminating is a story told by Gudmund Frunck about Samuel Hedborn (1783-1849) and Sofia Maria Levin.[31] Hedborn was a poet and hymn-writer, a minor member of the Romantic group, who had lived as a tutor in the house of Sofia Levin when she was fourteen years old. She was an unusual girl certainly: allegedly acquainted with most German books—"hardly any was unknown to her"— she knew *Genoveva* by heart and liked that the best. She was reprimanded for being *"en liten katolik,"* with Catholic sympathies received from *Maria Stuart* and *Genoveva.* Hedborn thought she adopted the opinions of others too much—

a tendency hardly unnatural in a girl of fourteen—and added, rather significantly, that her Catholic feelings were held not only by her but by many of her admirers.[32] As for Hedborn himself, he imagined, in a song of May 2, 1808, his own and Atterbom's death and burial in a Catholic temple, for a grave in such a hallowed place would be most welcome.

However, this was probably not to be taken too seriously, and Frunck cannot in the youthful utterings see any real Catholic religiosity. The Romanticists just had to talk about some mythology or other, he explains, and, after all, the Catholic one was the closest, for we had had both pagan and Catholic forefathers. This was good reasoning from a modern viewpoint, but many of the contemporary observers regarded the matter quite differently. Of the twenty sonnets written by Atterbom in 1810 and published in *Phosphoros,* one, "Saint Birgitta on Her Deathbed," was taken by *Allmänna Journalen,* 1817 (No. 63), to indicate glorification of Catholicism and monkery.[33] In general the Swedish Romanticists did not, however, object to being accused of Catholic leanings so long as they were not called *papists.* They distinguished carefully between Catholicism and papism. It was, then, often a mere case of religious government, authority. They probably would not worship the head of any church who was a foreigner. It was in part a matter of patriotism.

For several decades after the end of the Romantic revolt in Sweden, the criticism of the New School in literary history had often been severe. Then, in 1880, appeared *Nya Skolan Bedömd i Litteraturhistorien,* by Börje Norling, which was in tone exceedingly friendly, though in some places a bit naïve and puerile. Considerable space is devoted to the controversial subject of Catholicism. Norling accuses Fryxell, Malmström, and others of distortion of facts, mutilation and displacement of quotations, and general misinterpretation. He agrees with the Phosphorists that there was nothing wrong in singing the praises of the Holy Virgin, provided that it was not actual *worship*; that it was not idolatry. On the other hand, he believes that the members of the more national Gothic School in Sweden, who lauded Thor and Odin, could with greater reason be termed idolaters. The New School in its Madonna cult did what any good Christians should do. "It is true," says Norling, "that the New School has left a type of defense of Catholicism, but it has done so from a purely historical viewpoint; without being champions of Catholic teachings its members have understood fully the importance of Catholicism *in its place and time*."[34] Only fanatics can deny the former power and mission of Catholicism, the fanatics who talk of tolerance, meaning, of course, tolerance toward themselves. Any church has a right to defend itself—as noted above—yet Palmblad believed, as Norling emphasizes, that force should be used only when a sect arises which threatens to overthrow religion completely. Catholicism was the right religion for the Middle Ages, when feeling governed the ignorant masses. The Phosphorists, he declares, never defended "*det på avvägar stadda katolicism.*"[35] They had, to be sure, expressed the idea that the Reformation was or should be dissolved, but not Protestantism. Norling is weak in his discussion of the Reformation issue, and his charge of misinterpretation on the part of former critics is not too convincing; certainly the *form* of the Swedish adulation for Virgin Mary might well in some Lutheran circles be considered cause for criticism.

Our strongest critical evidence in the problem of Catholic inclinations is the fact that a whole century after the polemic feuds between the Old and the New School in Sweden were over—when the old animosities had died and unprejudiced students of the matter could afford to be sane and objective—most literary historians still admitted the existence of Catholic tendencies.

THE PROBLEM OF CATHOLIC SYMPATHIES IN SWEDISH ROMANTICISM

Henrik Schück, the late nonagenarian dean of Swedish literary history, asserted in 1918, not only that New Romanticism in Sweden was a sworn opponent of materialism, but that it was orthodox and "even felt a strong attraction for medieval Catholicism."[36] The New Romanticists, says Schück, raved about the Italian Renaissance literature, particularly Ariosto, to whom Wieland in Germany had called attention, and then turned to Spain, where especially Calderon's "burning Catholicism and knightly ultra-royalism" appealed to the New-Romantic taste.[37] Richard Steffen, 1919, readily admits, also, that the Swedish Romanticists were in some degree attracted by Catholicism, and that the chief reason for the decline of religion, in their opinion, was the Reformation's defection from the "only saving [Catholic] Church."[38] Fredrik Böök feels that the above-named translation by Palmblad of a "Hymn to the Holy Virgin" was of significance, although the translator, he suspects, may have been more interested in the external form of poetry than in the Virgin herself.[39]

Henrik Schück's final review and summary of the Swedish Romantic School in the third edition of Schück-Warburg's monumental *Illustrerad Svensk Litteraturhistoria*[40] pays appropriate attention to its Catholic propensities, although his former collaborator had practically denied them.[41] Schück, in speaking of Atterbom's initiation address to the Musis Amici Society, mentions particularly the latter's conjuring up of a temple with the Madonna on a front portal. Atterbom, he reports, attacked the "rational Protestants" who—quoting Atterbom—had "mocked the Almighty God and sullied the light angel-features of poetry, which on earth comprised the mystical image of the heavenly Maria. The frigid Protestants would probably, like himself, kneel down before the Holy Mother and her Child, and accompanied by organ tones stammer forth their repentance." Then follows in

Schück's review Atterbom's sonnet to the Holy Virgin, beginning:

> O helga Jungfru! I ditt öra skalla
> En mängd af suckar ifrån jordens söner.
> Ur glorian, som din gudahjässa kröner,
> Jag vet du ser med modersblick dem alla.

Schück then devotes a whole page to an analysis of the Catholic tendency.[42] He emphasizes that the Romanticists had fought for imagination, and it was therefore natural that there should, both in Germany and Sweden, be "a certain sympathy for Catholicism." This was from the beginning apparent in the Aurora Society which initiated and sponsored the Romantic ideals, and was continued in the writings of its members even after 1809. Many Germans had turned Catholic, he reminds us, but Swedish converts would probably at that time have been exiled. Schück agrees with Wallmark, the polemic opponent of the New School, that the Phosphorists cherished a *svärmeri* for the Holy Virgin, saints, and cloisters that was "not entirely Protestant." Palmblad could easily prove that he and his friends were not papists, but he could not deny his friendly attitude toward several aspects of Catholicism. Then he takes up another matter.

Atterbom had in 1816 joined the polemic battle between the contending factions and claimed, among other things, that the teachings of the New School were taught in the academic halls of the University of Uppsala. The theological faculty was up in arms over the contention, the Archbishop became agitated, there was much deliberation, and a definite denial that such teaching was taking place; so in the end nothing was done about it. It is said that the Crown Prince Karl Johan (Bernadotte) had interfered in the proceedings, claiming that public authorities were always wrong when they entered into philosophical discussions. (In any event, the Archbishop was probably glad that the Ro-

THE PROBLEM OF CATHOLIC SYMPATHIES IN SWEDISH ROMANTICISM

manticists remained Christians, whatever their transgressions.) And Ingelgren, for instance, though he leaned towards Catholicism, was not a dangerous militant devotee. Hedborn, a sincere Christian, had in fact, little of the Catholic about him.

An extraordinary, independent Romanticist of notable creative accomplishments, who did not formally join any School but chose his own program, was the young gnostic, epic, and dramatic poet Erik Johan Stagnelius (1793-1823). He dealt in two outstanding works with a typical Catholic background, but was regarded as being so exclusively poetic that none of the Old School academicians dared charge him with Catholicism. He had never taken part in the polemic and philosophical squabbles of the time. The productions in question were the "antiquating epos" *Wladimir den Store* ("Wladimir the Great"), 1817, in classical hexameters, and the Christian tragedy *Martyrerna* ("Martyrs"). The former dealt with a Russian Grand Duke, who in an atmosphere of saints, cloisters, hermits, revelations, and what Schück calls "bigoted Catholicism," is converted to Christianity by the Greek Princess Anna. In the unified state of medieval times Stagnelius saw the ideal community. The poet here gave the expression of the young generation for its reactionary political views and religious enthusiasm. *Martyrerna*, externally a tragedy, is based on Chateaubriand's *Les Martyrs* and *Le Génie du Christianisme*, and reminds one strongly of Corneille's *Polyeucte*. The Roman Perpetua has become a Christian, is discovered and condemned to death, and yearningly suffers martyrdom, despite the frantic dissuasions of her relatives, whose feelings are totally disregarded. Even her parents are sacrificed in the fanatic determination to die for her faith. Critics have noted that since Perpetua longs for death, there is no real tragic conflict, no terror: death is her only hope and greatest achievement. Stagnelius obviously was intensely interested in the era and philosophy of martyrs. The Christians in the drama are "hard, prejudiced, and frightfully bigoted";[43] and the pagans represent humanity.

A perusal and checking of the pages of the bi-weekly *Polyfem* and the monthly *Phosphoros* fails to disclose much additional information: the hostile critics of the New School had from the beginning raked the field with a fine-toothed comb. In fact, we suspect that once at least they had in their rakings collected more than they should have. Certainly the *Polyfem* article on charity (*Tredje Samlingen* [III], Nos. 38 and 39), criticized by Malmström, could well have been written without serious thoughts of the Catholic countries. And, in *Polyfem* Luther is treated with great respect (IV, 6). Nevertheless, we find a few statements in the journal which are vulnerable to attack from a Protestant standpoint. For example, take this sentence translated from Novalis: "The original personal hatred of the Catholic faith, gradually passed over into a hatred of the Bible, of the Christian faith, and, finally, of all religion" (III, 24). The declared mysticism and Catholicism in Schelling's philosophy is indirectly defended (III, 32); a contributor cites the method of the establishment of universities in former days as examples of the "highest and truly wise spirit which prevailed during the Middle Ages" (IV, 34); and in a discussion on new literary education the writer admits that many had found it "highly serious in our day to discover the Holy Virgin, saints, and angels in our poems" (IV, 43).

In *Phosphoros* for 1810 we find, with some surprise, a warm recognition of Luther for his contribution to choral song (p. 55); translations from Tasso (pp. 74 ff. and 160 ff.), which were to be expected; and a reference to the "sacred twilight of Catholicism" (p. 166). Further on we are reminded (p. 186) that "when the knight of old consecrated his sword to the Mother of God, the Empress of Heaven, he swore through her to protect all women."

Phosphoros for 1812-13 informs us, in a dialogue on the novel, that the power of imagination emanated from "the throne of Mary, from King Arthur, and the Holy Sepulchre" (p. 117); and (p. 168) speaks of the "severity of Protestantism and the lovable freedom of Catholicism." Later we learn about the "Catholic Christianism" in the growth of religious development, and in Atterbom's "Epilogue" we welcome, again, the "immortal charm of God's Mother" (p. 387).

Re-examining *Poetisk Kalender*, which had superseded *Phosphoros* as the literary organ of the Romanticists, we find in the double number for 1814-15 nothing objectionable from the rigidly Protestant viewpoint; a few sonnets only in imitation of Petrarch recall a German and south European influence. The volume for 1816, however, one of ballads and romances, has not only the unobjectionable and ubiquitous St. George and the dragon, with the rescued maiden, but the tale of a king's daughter and a flower-master who turns out to be the Lord Jesus in person, and who tells of His mother, "the holy Mary." The environment is, of course, wholly medieval. Of some consequence are certain parts of Atterbom's Foreword to this volume of "unpublished ancient songs (*fornsånger*), which go far back to Catholic times." ... And "it is not my intention," says Atterbom, "as so many seem to believe, to re-introduce the Asa mythology or Catholicism,[44] either seriously or superficially [*blott uniforms-vis*], as some of our recent [Swedish] poets have done, making use of our forefathers' myths and names of divinities. At least it is not *my* intention...."[45]—It was then, in other words, merely a poetic and historical display. Yet appearances in his works were often against him, exhibiting as they did, a fondness for knights, princesses, evidences of the Cross, saints, and the previously quoted maxim of "all hearts beating for Christus and Maria."[46] There was yet, in 1816, a definite Un-Lutheran emphasis on Holy Mary.

Still, in a sense, the Foreword was historical, evolutionary: Vikingism was followed by chivalry and Catholicism, it said; all were parts of a development for something higher; yet, even Catholicism must disappear, "although several of its ideas, such as that of the Holy Virgin, are based on eternal truths,"[47] for everything of a sensuous form of truth that is subject to natural laws must sooner or later disappear.

The *Poetisk Kalender* for 1820 contains many poems from Atterbom's visit to Italy, including "The Fair Nun" (*Den sköna nunnan*), dated at Albano, August, 1818; and "On the Heights of Olebano," whence he hears the sound of cloister bells ascending to Mary:

Från klostret fjerran till Maria flyr
Vid solens afsked bedjande klockans klang... (August 24, 1818).

He recalls, in a different meter, Dante, Beatrice, and others. In the same volume we find "The Rome-Farer's Spring" (*Romfars källa*, by "Euphrosyne," Julia Nyberg, a minor Romantic poet), a popular legend from the province of Västmanland, which relates the miracle of a spring gushing forth at the place of execution of an innocent victim. It is the story of a pilgrim, who, inspired by St. Peter's Church in Rome and the gift of a chalice from the Pope himself, returns to his native land to erect a temple. The chalice, however, later mysteriously disappears; it is discovered in Romfar's belongings, whereupon he is, wrongly, accused of the theft and executed. There are three legends in the *Kalender* for 1821, and among them is a similar one, by Atterbom, "Sanct Ranghild," apparently a variation of the theme treated by Palmblad,[48] which describes the martyrship of an innocent girl unjustly accused by a cloister abbess of sin: a spring issues forth on the spot of martyrdom.

The last number of *Poetisk Kalender,* 1822, continues much

in the same vein. Here "Euphrosyne" has published the legend of Christopheros, about a hero, Reprobus, who sets out to find the greatest king in the universe. He learns that "the Holy Mother" is "his best friend," and that the image of the Holy Virgin is above the portal of a certain royal castle. In a Romantic atmosphere of owls, wolves, and hermits, Reprobus is urged by one of the latter to be humble, is finally baptized as a Christian, and discovers that Christ is the greatest king. The volume contains also a number of "Evangelical Romances" in verse on Jesus Christ, by "Carl" (Carl von Zeipel), dealing with the annunciation and the birth and early life of Jesus, all based on the Gospels. There are nineteen poems in the cycle, in various meters, and somehow we cannot help feeling, when reading them, that the central figure is Mary rather than Jesus. In any case, her position in the cycle is, naturally, at least equivalent to that of her Son.

Our conclusions may be summarized briefly. There existed for approximately fifteen years, from about 1807 to 1822, among a few leaders of the New School in Swedish Romanticism, a definite sympathy for certain aspects of Catholicism, whether we call it poetic, esthetic, symbolic, historical, or philosophical. This sympathy was expressed in *words,* both in verse and prose, and not in *radical action,* and generally in eulogies of the Holy Virgin. The latter proved harmless to the Lutheran State Church. Freedom of the press, as by enactment of March 13, 1809, facilitated, without serious consequences, discussions of all subjects for all parties concerned. For half a century or more, beginning about 1810, critics and literary historians overemphasized the importance of the Catholic tendency and were unnecessarily bitter in their denunciations. The number of Catholicizing Swedish Romanticists was, however, relatively small, and probably only Atterbom had anything more than a temporary feeling and admiration for the beauties of Catholicism or Holy Mary. No

Swede joined the Catholic Church at the time, at least not in Sweden: if he had, he could have been and possibly would have been exiled. Actually, the pro-Catholic writings, as we may call them, of the Phosphorists were in proportion to their total critical and creative output quantitatively insignificant, although we can easily understand why some Protestants were, for a time, disturbed. Yet, even from *their* viewpoint no permanent damage was done, possibly in part because the Romantic works often were too obscure to be understood by the general public

REFERENCES

1. Henrik Schück and Karl Warburg, *Illustrerad Svensk Litteratur-Historia*, Andra Upplagan, Tredje Delen, Stockholm, 1913, p. 198.
2. E. N. Tigerstedt, *Svensk Litteraturhistoria*, Stockholm, 1948, p. 246.
3. *The Old Norse Element in Swedish Romanticism*, New York, 1914.
4. *Bidrag till Sveriges Litteratur-Historia*, 1-9, Stockholm, 1860-62.
5. *Ibid.*, 1, 10.
6. "Här visades på samma ovedersägliga sätt, att fosforisterna röjde en icke obetvdlig benägenhet för åtskilliga katolska åsigter." *Ibid.*, 2, 103.
7. "Heljsan! Religionen är Jesuit,
Meniskorätt Jakobin.
Verlden är fri, och korpen är hvit,
Vivat påfven och Hin!"
8. *Ibid.*, 4, 3.
9. *Ibid.*, 4, 15.
10. *Poetisk Kalender*, 1816, LXIII.
11. Fryxell, *ibid.*, 4, 16, and *Svensk Litteratur-Tidning*, 1821, Nos. 35 and 36.
12. Albert Nilsson, *Svensk Romantik*, Lund, 1916, pp. 183 ff.
13. Fryxell, *op. cit.*, 4, 16, quoted from *Svensk Litteratur-Tidning*, 1814, 458.
14. Fryxell, *op. cit.*, 4, 17, quoted from its Romantic source.
15. *Ibid.*
16. *Grunddragen af Svenska Vitterhetens Historia*, Femte Delen, Örebro, 1868. *Striden Mellan Gamla och Nya Skolan*.
17. *Ibid.*, p. 82.
18. *Ibid.*, p. 83.
19. *Ibid.*, pp. 240 ff.
20. *Ibid.*, p. 245.
21. *Svensk Litteratur-Tidning*, 1818, 27-28.
22. Pp. 386-89; 439-40.
23. *Grunddragen af Svenska Vitterhetens Historia*, Fjerde Delen, pp. 457-59.
24. See Fjerde Delen, Lund, 1890. All references are to this part.
25. *Ibid.*, p. 17.
26. *Ibid.*, p. 42, quoted from Atterbom.
27. *Ibid.*, p. 44.
28. *Ibid.*, p. 44.
29. *Ibid.*, p. 44.

THE PROBLEM OF CATHOLIC SYMPATHIES IN SWEDISH ROMANTICISM

30. *Ibid.*, p. 540. *Phosphoros*, 1813, p. 375.
31. Gudmund Frunck, *Bidrag till Kännedom om Nya Skolans Förberedelser och Första Utveckling* (till år 1811), Stockholm, 1889, pp. 44, with note, and 45.
32. *Ibid.*, p. 45.
33. *Ibid.*, p. 198.
34. Börje Norling, *Nya Skolan*, p. 258.
35. *Ibid.*, p. 260. The Swedish means "Catholicism gone astray."
36. *Huvuddragen av Sveriges Litteratur*, Tredje avdelningen, p. 50.
37. *Ibid.*, p. 53.
38. Richard Steffen, *Svensk Litteraturhistoria*, Stockholm, 1919, p. 157.
39. *Den Romantiska Tidsåldren i Svenska Litteraturens Historia*, 1919, Andra Delen, p. 134.
40. Femte Delen, 1929, pp. 17. ff.
41. See above, p. 139.
42. V, pp. 81-82.
43. Henrik Schück, *Huvuddragen av Sveriges Litteratur*, Trejde Avdelningen, 1918, p. 83.
44. See above, p. 152.
45. *Poetisk Kalender* for 1816, p. xxvii.
46. See note 10.
47. *Ibid.*, pp. xxxi-xxxii.
48. See above, p. 150.

[161]

Albert Morey Sturtevant:

BIBLIOGRAPHY OF PUBLICATIONS

L. R. LIND

University of Kansas

Abbreviations: *AJP*—American Journal of Philology; *Germ. Rev.*—The Germanic Review; *JEGP*—The Journal of English and Germanic Philology; *Lang.*—Language; *MLN*—Modern Language Notes; *MP*—Modern Philology; *PMLA*—Publications of the Modern Language Association; *PQ*—Philological Quarterly; *SSN (SS)*—Scandinavian Studies and Notes, later Scandinavian Studies; *SP*—Studies in Philology.

1910

Zur Sprache des Peter von Suchenwirt; *MLN*. 25. 47-51.
Ibsen's *Peer Gynt* and *Paa Vidderne; JEGP.* 9. 43-48.

1911

The Relation of Loddfáfnir to Odin in the *Hávamál; JEGP.* 10. 42-55.

1912

A Note on the Impersonal Pronoun in Old High German; *MLN*. 27. 1-5.
A Type of Ellipsis in Old Norse; *ibid*. 75-78.
Olaf Liljekrans and Ibsen's Later Works; *JEGP.* 11. 381-401.
Three Notes on Ibsen's *Peer Gynt; SSN.* 1. 27-37.

1913

Altnordisch *Tryggr; MLN*. 28. 161-163.
Zum Reimgebrauch Otfrids; *ibid*. 239-243.
Kjæmpehøien and Its Relation to Ibsen's Romantic Works; *JEGP.* 12. 407-424.
A Note on the *Hárbarðsljóð; SSN.* 1. 157-164.

1914

Aase and Peer Gynt; *MLN*. 29. 233-239.
A Study of the Old Norse Word *Mein; SSN.* 1. 221-250.
Some Phases of Ibsen's Symbolism; *ibid*. 2. 25-50.

1915

Ibsen's *Sankthansnatten; JEGP.* 14. 357-374.
A Note on the *Sigrdrifumál; SSN.* 2. 79-91.
Rev. of E. Classen, *On Vowel Alliteration in the Old Germanic Languages; MLN*. 30. 108-114.
Rev. of A. B. Benson, *The Old Norse Element in Swedish Romanticism; ibid*. 227-229.

BIBLIOGRAPHY OF PUBLICATIONS

1916
Zur Syntax des Verbums *meinen* im Althochdeutschen; *MLN*. 31. 85-90.
A Study of the Old Norse Word *Regin*; *JEGP*. 15. 251-266.
Pessimism in Tegnér's Poetry; *SSN*. 3. 112-133.
Semological Notes on Old Norse *Heim-* in Compounds; *ibid*. 253-264.

1917
Zum Gotischen Dativ nach *waírþan* mit Infinitiv; *MLN*. 32. 141-151.
Über Neubildungen bei Altnordischem *Friósa* und *Kjósa; JEGP*. 16. 499-514.
Bjørnson's *Maria Stuart i Skotland; SSN*. 4. 203-219.

1918
Über die Stellung des Starken Attributiven Adjektivs im Deutschen; *JEGP*. 17. 329-345.
Olaf Liljekrans and Ibsen's Literary Development; *SSN*. 5. 110-132.
Rev. of J. Lassen, *Ein Volksfeind; JEGP*. 17. 439-448.

1919
Zur *A*-Brechung im Nord- und Westgermanischen; *JEGP*. 18. 378-401.
The Family in Bjørnson's Tales; *ibid*. 607-627.
Romantic Elements in Tegnér's Religious Philosophy; *SSN*. 5. 213-245.

1920
Tegnér's *Gerda*; *SSN*. 6. 43-57.
Tegnér's Poetic Treatment of Death; *ibid*. 93-112.

1921
Zum Vokalismus des Gotischen *Waihando*, Röm. 7: 23; *JEGP*. 20. 22-27.
Zum Altnordischen Vokalismus; *ibid*. 513-538.
Die Endung des Partizipium Präteriti der Germanischen Starken Verben; *AJP*. 42. 12-24.
Oehlenschläger and Tegnér's *Frithiofs saga; SSN*. 6. 134-159.
Rev. of D. A. Seip, *Norsk Sproghistorie*; *JEGP*. 20. 399-403.

1922
Gothic Notes; *JEGP*. 21. 442-456.
The Character of Ingeborg in Tegnér's *Frithiofs saga; SSN*. 7. 31-51.
Tegnér's *Frithiof på sin faders hög; ibid*. 102-109.
Rev. of Hjalmar Falk, *Betydningslære*; *JEGP*. 21. 171-178.

1923
Die Behandlung der Lautgruppen *WE* and *WA* bei den altnordischen starken Verben; *JEGP*. 22. 245-252.
The Relation of Old Norse *-rð-* to Gothic *-rd-*; *ibid*. 369-375.
The Irregular Declension of the Old Norse Noun *mær*, 'Maiden'; *SSN*. 7. 169-174.

BIBLIOGRAPHY OF PUBLICATIONS

Regarding "Subconscious Elements in the Composition of *Peer Gynt*"; *ibid*. 201-207.
The Cultural Elements in Bjørnson's *Fiskerjænten* with Special Reference to Goethe's *Wilhelm Meister*; *ibid*. 257-264.

1924

Old Norse Semasiological and Etymological Notes; *SSN*. 8. 37-47.
Regarding the Nominative Singular Ending *-r* in Old Norse; *ibid*. 80-83.
Berthold Auerbach's *Die feindlichen Brüder* and Bjørnson's Story of the Two Brothers, Bård and Anders, in *En Glad Gut*: a Comparison; *ibid*. 142-150.
Old Norse *Sko*; *MLN*. 39. 378-379.
Hiatuserscheinungen im Altisländischen; *ibid*. 40. 25-29.
Fíu, Runische Form für Altisländisches *Fé*; *JEGP*. 23. 512-515.
Old Norse *-ðr* from *-*nn+r*; *ibid*. 23. 78-82.
Rev. of George T. Flom, *The Language of the Konungs Skuggsjá*, Part II; *SSN*. 8. 156-163.

1925

Regarding Circumlocutions in the Elder Edda; *MLN*. 11. 216-219.
Old Saxon Notes; *ibid*. 11. 399-404.
Gotisch *lasiws* 'Opportunus'; *JEGP*. 24. 195-196.
Gotica; *ibid*. 24. 504-511.
Old Norse Notes; *SSN*. 8. 199-209.
Rev. of Iversen, *Norrøn Grammatikk*; *JEGP*. 24. 144-154.
Rev. of Small, *The Comparison of Inequality*; *MLN*. 11. 492-501.

1926

Zum Fugenvokal in Westgermanischen Kompositis; *MLN*. 41. 189-193.
Some Old Norse Etymologies; *ibid*. 370-375.
The Imperative Use of the Gothic Infinitive *haban* in Luke, 9: 3; *ibid*. 382-384.
Gotica; *JEGP*. 24. 504-511.
Some Old Norse Etymologies; *ibid*. 25. 216-226.
Bjørnson's *Mors Hænder*; *SSN*. 8. 249-257.
Notes on Tegnér's Posthumous Poems; *ibid*. 9. 1-12.
Notes on the Poetic Edda; *ibid*. 9. 31-36.
Ägir and the Magic Ship *Ellida* in Tegnér's *Frithiofs saga*; *ibid*. 9. 56-60.

1927

Some Etymologies of Certain Old Norse Words Dealing with the Supernatural; *SSN*. 9. 151-159.
Gleanings from *Peer Gynt*; *ibid*. 9. 224-230.
The Suffix *-erni* in Old Norse; *ibid*. 9. 267-270.
Old Icelandic Notes; *Germ. Rev.* 2. 64-74.
Zum Lautwandel *æ*: *ió*: *iá*: im Altnordischen; *ibid*. 2. 334-352.

BIBLIOGRAPHY OF PUBLICATIONS

Initial *h* before *l, n, r*, in Old Icelandic: a Type of Associative Consonant Groups; *Lang.* 3. 169-174.
Some Adverbial Formations in Old Norse; *MP.* 25. 137-147.

1928

Notes on the Substitution of the *j*-Suffix for the *v*-Suffix in the Old Norse Verb; *SSN.* 10. 26-30.
Old Norse *tig-inn*: *tíg-inn*; *fú-inn*: *lú-inn*; *ibid.* 10. 50-55.
Some Critical Notes on Bjørnson's *Halte Hulda*; *ibid.* 10. 79-86.
Zum *u*-Umlaut im Nordischen; *JEGP.* 27. 67-82.
Altnordisch *tigr; ibid.* 27. 371-382.
Two Notes on the Gothic Text; *PQ.* 7. 78-82.
The Use of the Weak Inflection of the Gothic Adjective in a Vocative Function; *ibid.* 7. 199-206.
A Note on the Gothic Particle *þau*; *MLN.* 43. 242-244.
Some Vowel Variations in Certain Old Norse Words; *SP.* 25. 376-384.
The Suffix *-sk-* in Old Norse *elska; AJP.* 49. 188-195.
The Consonant *þ* in Gothic *stôþ*: *stôþum*; *Lang.* 4. 109-110.
Certain Old Norse Suffixes; *MP.* 26. 149-159.
Rev. of Jóhannesson, *Die Suffixe im Isländischen*; *SSN.* 10. 89-92.

1929

Old Norse Preterite Present Verbs with Past Participles in *-at; SSN.* 10. 147-148.
Notes on the *A*-Umlaut in Old Norse; *ibid.* 203-205.
The Women Characters in Ibsen's *Samfundets Støtter*: a Comparison with the Earlier Versions of the Play; *ibid.* 231-237.
Certain Old Norse Suffixes; *MP.* 26. 467-476.

1930

Regarding the *u*-Ending in Old Norse *vett-u-gis; vett-u-gi; SSN.* 11. 29-30.
Notes on Old Norse Weak Contracted Verbs Derived from Strong Verbs; *ibid.* 61-63.
Notes on Alexander L. Kielland; *ibid.* 90-99.
Regarding the Connective Vowel *-i-* in Old Norse Compounds; *ibid.* 125-127.
Die Altnordische Senkung *i:u > e:o* vor *kk, pp, tt; AJP.* 51. 42-50.
Old Norse Phonological Notes; *JEGP.* 29. 237-242.
Gothic Syntactical Notes; *Studies in Honor of Hermann Collitz*, 101-113.
Some Critical Notes on Old Norse Phonology; *Lang.* 6. 253-263.

1931

Gothic Notes; *Germ. Rev.* 6. 54-68.
Altnordisch *verr*: *verri*; *ibid.* 6. 294-298.
Old Norse Phonological Notes; *SSN.* 11. 180-182.
Old Norse Phonological Notes; *ibid.* 11. 206-208.

Skipper Worse and the Haugianere; *ibid.* 11. 229-239.
Shift of Spirant to Stop in a Combination of Two Spirants in North and West Germanic; *Lang.* 7. 190-193.
Notes on Old Norse Phonology; *JEGP.* 30. 155-164.

1932

Old Norse Phonological Notes; *SSN.* 12. 10-13; 36-39.
Notes on the Consonantal Stems in Old Norse; *JEGP.* 31. 247-250.
Notes on the *X*-Sinking in Old Norse; *ibid.* 407-490.
The Lengthening of Vowels before *-tt*<*-χt* in Old Norse; *Lang.* 8. 215-216.
Gothic Notes; *AJP.* 53. 53-60.
Germanic Notes; *Germ. Rev.* 7. 367-373.

1933

Regarding the Chronology of Events in Kielland's Novels; *SSN.* 12. 101-109.
Gotica; *Germ. Rev.* 8. 206-212.
Gothic Syntactical Notes; *AJP.* 54. 340-352.
Rev. of Cawley, *Hrafnkelssaga Freysgoða*; *MLN.* 48. 63 f.

1934

Old Norse Etymologies; *JEGP.* 33. 89-97.
Notes on Old Norse *R*; *Lang.* 9. 315-319.
Certain Phonetic Tendencies in Old Norse; *ibid.* 10. 17-26.
Rev. of Barber, *Die Vorgeschichtliche Betonung der Germanischen Substantiva und Adjektiva*; *ibid.* 10. 53-57.

1935

Old Saxon Notes; *AJP.* 56. 132-141.
Certain Analogical Changes in Old Norse; *JEGP.* 34. 180-187.
Old Norse Phonological Notes; *SSN.* 13. 69-72.
Old Norse Phonological Notes; *ibid.* 13. 81-85.
Rev. of Eikeland, *Ibsen Studies*; *ibid.* 13. 86-89.

1936

The Confusion of the Neuter *ia*-Declension with the Feminine *in*-Declension in Old Norse; *Lang.* 12. 45-47.
Germanic Notes; *JEGP.* 35. 389-400.
Gothic Miscellanies; *AJP.* 57. 271-285.

1937

Gothic Notes; *MLN.* 52. 207-209.
Gothic Semantic Notes; *JEGP.* 36. 176-182.

1938

Gothic Notes; *MLN.* 53. 120-122.

The Future Auxiliaries Gothic *Haban* and Old Norse *Munu; ibid.* 53. 423-425.
An Etymology of the Old Norse Word *Fljóð; SSN.* 15. 26-28.
Concerning Gothic Intransitive Verbs; *AJP.* 59. 460-470.
West Germanic Notes; *JEGP.* 37. 559-566.
The Use of Colors in the Elder Edda; *Germ. Rev.* 13. 289-299.

1939

A Derivation of the Old Norse Word *Vǫrð*, a Poetic Designation for 'Woman'; *SSN.* 15. 158-159.
A Study of Tegnér's Personality and Views as Revealed in His *Skoltal*; *ibid.* 15. 173-197.
The Shift of Gender in the Old Icelandic Words for the Seasons of the Year; *ibid.* 15. 275-278.
Collective Plurals in the Elder Edda; *Germ. Rev.* 14. 126-137.
The Doublets Old Icelandic *skyti:skytja*, 'Shooter, Marksman'; *MLN.* 54. 445-447.
Rev. of Heinrichs, *Stilbedeutung des Adjektivs im eddischen Liede*; *SSN.* 15. 284-285.

1940

Analogical Weak Preterite Forms in Old Icelandic; *Lang.* 16. 48-52.
Analogical Formations in Old Norse; *ibid.* 16. 160-161.
Critical Notes on Old Norse Phonology; *ibid.* 16. 344-346.
Gothic *þis*; *MLN.* 55. 599-601.
The Position of the Verb-Adverb Locution with Reference to the Verb in the Elder Edda; *SSN.* 16. 1-21.
Certain Aspects of Tegnér's Views Concerning Poetry; *ibid.* 16. 68-78.
Four Notes on Tegnér's *Mjältsjukan*; *ibid.* 16. 128-132.
Gothic Notes; *JEGP.* 39. 456-461.
Rev. of Sherwin, *The Viking and the Red Man: The Old Norse Origin of the Algonquin Language*; *SSN.* 16. 114-116.

1941

An American Appreciation of Esaias Tegnér; *SS.* 16. 157-164.
A Note on the Semantic Development of Old Norse *frjá*; *ibid.* 16. 194-196.
Some Etymologies of Old Norse Poetic Words; *ibid.* 16. 220-225.
Semantic and Etymological Notes on Old Norse Words Pertaining to War; *ibid.* 16. 257-263.
The Neuter Gender of Old Norse *Fljóð* and *Sprund*; *Lang.* 17. 255-256.
Rev. of Wood, *Eddic Lays*; *SS.* 197-200.

1942

Esaias Tegnér's Poem *Till H. M. Konung Karl XIV Johan*: an Appreciative Analysis; *SS.* 17. 36-42.
Some Poetic Synonyms of Prose Words in the Elder Edda; *ibid.* 17. 114-115.

BIBLIOGRAPHY OF PUBLICATIONS

Old Norse Philological Notes; *Illinois Studies in Language and Literature.* 29. 49-53.

1943

Notes on Verner's Law in Old Norse Strong Verbs; *MLN.* 58. 27-28.
A Note on the *u*-Declension in Old Norse; *ibid.* 58. 454-455.
Notes on Old Norse Philology; *SS.* 17. 157-166.
Certain Aspects of Tegnér's Poetic Art; *ibid.* 17. 204-211.
Some Critical Notes on Tegnér's Poetry; *ibid.* 17. 238-247.
Notes on Words in the Elder Edda; *ibid.* 17. 282-289.
Old Norse Philological Notes; *JEGP.* 42. 539-550.

1944

An Appreciative Approach to Tegnér's Poetic Technique; *SS.* 18. 1-13.
Old Norse Philological Notes; *ibid.* 18. 61-70.
Repetition of Metaphors in Tegnér's Poetry; *ibid.* 18. 125-137.
Regarding the Prefix *ý-* in Old Norse *ý-miss; MLN.* 59. 175-176.

1945

Gothic Syntactical Notes; *MLN.* 60. 104-106.
Notes on the Text of the Gothic Bible; *JEGP.* 44. 62-65.
Concerning Irregular Forms in Gothic; *ibid.* 44. 370-377.
Notes on Gothic Morphology; *PMLA.* 60. 1-9.
Regarding Personifications in Tegnér's Poetry; *SS.* 18. 241-248.
Notes on Tegnér's *Frithiofs saga; ibid.* 18. 252-260.
Regarding Discrepancies in Tegnér's Poetry; *ibid.* 18. 261-268.

1946

Notes on Certain Old Norse Analogical Forms; *MLN.* 61. 57-60.
Semantic Notes on the Elder Edda; *SS.* 19. 1-18.
Irregularities in the Old Norse Substantive Declensions; *ibid.* 19. 79-88.
Rev. of Hesselman, *Omljud och brytning i de nordiska språken; JEGP.* 45. 346-352.

1947

Some Irregular Forms in Old Norse; *MLN.* 62. 255-258.
Some Irregular Preterite Forms in Old Norse; *SS.* 19. 173-180.
Notes on Old Norse Phonology; *ibid.* 19. 208-216.
An Analysis of Certain Metaphors in Tegnér's Poetry; *ibid.* 19. 270-277.
Gothic Morphological Notes; *JEGP.* 46. 92-97.
Gothic Syntactical Notes; *ibid.* 46. 407-412.

1948

The Derivations of Old Norse *Hǫlkvir* and *Fǫlkvir,* Poetic Designations for *Horse*; *MLN.* 63. 128-130.
Esaias Tegnér's *Den döde,* a Love Poem; SS. 20. 25-28.
Gleanings from Tegnér's Poetry; *ibid.* 20. 29-30.

Possible Traces of Ibsen's Influence upon Bjørnson; *ibid.* 20. 92-95.
Semantic and Etymological Notes on Old Norse Poetic Works; *ibid.* 20. 129-142.
Tegnér's Literary Activity during the Period 1840-1846; *ibid.* 20. 202-208.
Old Norse Syntactical Notes; *PMLA.* 63. 712-717.

1949

Certain Problems in Old Norse Phonology; *SS.* 21. 36-45.
Some Old Norse Phonological Problems; *ibid.* 21. 92-100.
Notes on Certain Gothic Forms; *Germ. Rev.* 24. 136-142.
Etymologies of Old Norse Proper Names Used as Poetic Designations; *MLN.* 64. 486-490.
Rev. of Krahe, *Historische Laut- und Formenlehre des Gotischen*; *JEGP.* 48. 379-384.

1950

Certain Gothic Cruxes; *JEGP.* 49. 78-87.
Three Old Norse Etymologies; *SS.* 22. 51-56.

1951

Miscellaneous Gothic Notes; *Germ. Rev.* 26. 50-59.
Etymological Comments on Certain Words and Names in the Elder Edda; *PMLA.* 46. 278-291.
Notes on Certain Variations and Forms in the Old Germanic Dialects; *MLN.* 66. 300-304.
Old Icelandic Phonetic and Semantic Notes; *SS.* 23. 60-72.
Certain Semantic Changes in Old Norse; *PQ.* 30. 308-315.
Rev. of Wolfgang Krause, *Abriss der Altwestnordischen Grammatik; Germ. Rev.* 26. 233-235.

1952

Comments on Certain Gothic Irregularities; *Germ. Rev.* 27. 50-55.

41388

ST. MARY'S COLLEGE OF MARYLAND
   ST. MARY'S CITY, MARYLAND